How to Publish your Poetry

Also by Peter Finch

Poetry
Wanted
Pieces of the Universe
Cycle of the Suns
Beyond the Silence
An Alteration in the Way I Breathe
The Edge of Tomorrow
The End of the Vision
whitesung
Antarktika
Trowch Eich Radio 'mlaen
Connecting Tubes
The O Poems
Blues & Heartbreakers
Some Music and a Little War
Reds in the Bed
Make
Poems For Ghosts

Fiction
Blats
Between 35 & 42

Other
Big Band Dance Music
Dances Interdites
Visual Texts 1970–1980
Getting Your Poetry Published
How To Publish Yourself
Publishing Yourself — Not Too Difficult After All

As Editor
Typewriter Poems
How to Learn Welsh
Green Horse (with Meic Stephens)

Peter Finch

How to Publish your Poetry

A practical guide

ALLISON & BUSBY

An Allison Busby Book
Published in 1991 by
W. H. Allen & Co. PLC
26 Grand Union Centre
338 Ladbroke Grove
London W10 5AH
3rd Revised Edition 1991

Copyright © 1985 by Peter Finch

Typeset by Medcalf Type Ltd, Bicester, Oxon
Printed and bound in Great Britain by
Cox & Wyman Ltd, Reading

British Library Cataloguing in Publication Data:

Finch, Peter, *1947–*
How to publish your poetry: a practical guide — 3rd ed.
1. Poetry — Publishing — Handbooks, manuals, etc.
I. Title
070.5'79   PN155

ISBN 0–85031–631–6

Contents

Acknowledgements 6

Introduction 7

1. You want to be a poet 9
2. Why write? 12
3. How good is it? 16
4. Publication — preparation of manuscripts 20
5. Sending it in 24
6. Markets — the individual poem 29
7. Rejection 37
8. The book-length manuscript 40
9. Markets — the book 48
10. Copyright 52
11. Cash 57
12. Doing it yourself 59
13. Actually doing it 64
14. What do you do with it next? 72
15. Vanity presses 79
16. Publishing abroad 84
17. Competitions 88
18. Readings and workshops 92
19. How to get better 96

Appendix 1: Bookshops 101
Appendix 2: Organizations of interest to poets 104
Appendix 3: The poet's library 114
Appendix 4: Books on publishing 116

Bibliography 117

Index 119

Acknowledgements

Unless otherwise stated, remarks in this book attributed to specific writers were made to the author in the course of his researches. Other copyright quotations come from the following, to whom full acknowledgement is made:

Michael Anania, Elliott Anderson and Mark Kinzie: *The Little Magazine in America*, Pushcart. Richard Findlater: *Authors' Earnings:* A Report in *The Author*, Summer 1982. John Haines: *Poets on Poetry — Living off the Country*, University of Michigan. Bill Henderson: *The Publish it Yourself Handbook*, Pushcart. Herman Hesse: *My Belief*, Panther. Norman Hidden: *How to be Your Own Publisher* and *How to Get Your Poems Accepted*, Workshop Press. Sarah Orne Jewett: *Letters of Sarah Orne Jewett*, edited by Annie Fields. Judson Jerome: *The Poet's Handbook*, Writer's Digest Books. Lotte Moos: *Time to be Bold*, Centerprise Trust Ltd. Jeff Nuttall in *PALPI*, ALP. Tillie Olsen: *Silences*, Virago. Ezra Pound: *Selected Poems*, Faber, and *Poetry (1916)*. Vernon Scannell: *How to Enjoy Poetry*, Piatkus. Michael Schmidt in *Poetry Wales*, Christopher Davies. Allan Sillitoe in *The Imagination on Trial*, edited by Alan Burns and Charles Sugnet, Allison and Busby. Stephan Themerson: *ALP Catalogue of Little Press Books in Print*, ALP. R.S. Thomas: *Selected Prose*, Poetry Wales Press. Edward Uhlan: *The Rogue of Publishers' Row*, Exposition Press. Sir Stanley Unwin: *The Truth About Publishing*, George Allen and Unwin Ltd.

(*Note:* Prices mentioned in this book are those current at the time of going to press.)

Introduction

How to Publish your Poetry grew out of the small pamphlet *Getting Your Poetry Published* which I compiled in 1973. I was editing a poetry magazine called *Second Aeon* at the time and was troubled by the amount of incorrectly submitted material continually arriving on my desk. A lot of people wanted to get published but they all seemed to be going about it the wrong way. Through talking to fellow editors and press operators it became apparent that this was not just my problem, it was endemic. What we needed was a ready printed booklet of answers we could send to our prospective contributors to help put them right. 37,000 copies and twelve revised editions later, the problem seems as big as it ever was.

The present volume attempts to advise both the novice — the newcomer to writing and publishing — as well as the poet who has already begun and is keen to carry on. It is not infallible, and it offers no guarantees or instant methods of success. But it will at least, if you read it all, give you a better chance.

In the course of its compilation I have surveyed with questionnaires, phone calls and letters a good many poets, publishers and magazine editors up and down the country. What I wanted was both a distillation of contemporary practices and something to help demystify the way in which poetry goes about its business. To all of those who bothered to reply to my pestering — and there were many — thank you. I have not quoted everyone but all the answers received were useful.

Special thanks are due to Bob Cobbing who, in the years after I finished magazine editing, kept me involved; and to Valerie, my wife, who suggested that as the subject was bigger than a pamphlet and the advice was still needed why didn't I write it up as a book. So despite the interruptions, phone calls, unavoidable engagements, late nights, important television shows and trips to the pub, here it is. Don't spend too long with it; use your time on your poems.

Peter Finch

1
You Want To Be a Poet

> I can well imagine a perfectly healthy society in which nobody
> reads poetry. I cannot imagine a healthy society in which nobody
> writes poetry.
> *Stephan Themerson*

So you want to be a poet. This book won't teach you. Far from it,
this is a guide to bettering your status — how to make it once you've
proved you can write, how to get on. If it is the craft that bothers
you, check the bibiliography; there may be something helpful there.
You might at first have hunted for a volume entitled *Getting a Job
in Poetry* or *Careers in Verse*. They don't exist. There would be little
point, there are no professional poets. There is probably no one at
all in Britain, Ireland or America who earns his or her living just
from the *writing* of verse. Tennyson might have sold 60,000 copies
a year of *In Memoriam A.H.H.* in the 1850s but a poet today is doing
wonderfully well to sell a tenth of that. The Poet Laureate gets a
nominal stipend and a gift of wine, the total value of which is less
than a hundred pounds. It is a mark of the commercial esteem in
which poets are held. My son by doing two paper-rounds can earn
more than that.

Yet poetry appears never to have been so popular. There were
40,000 entries to the last Arvon Foundation competition and almost
as many to the Poetry Society for its annual National contest.
Hundreds of thousands of people enter poetry competitions, further
thousands then send their poems to the poetry magazines. It is a
paradox which resists probing. Poetry is an esteemed art of impeccable
pedigree with a commercial status of nil. Norman Hidden, editor of
the now defunct journal *Workshop New Poetry* and author of a
number of books on poetry publishing, has concluded that:

> The whole of the "serious" poetry world is a commercially unviable,
> lovable, lunatic, totally "amateur" affair.

This surprises people. It shouldn't. Presumably you are reading
this book because you are interested in poetry, because it has come
to mean something in your life. Test yourself: write out the names
of all the contemporary poets you can think of. If you knew most,

your list would make a book. Oriel, the Welsh Arts Council's shop, has a catalogue of recent poetry which runs to 78 pages. Your list will be shorter, probably embarrassingly so. Put a tick against those whose books you've bought, not just recently but at all. Your ticks will be sparse. This is the rub, this is why financially most poetry fails.

For a long time the A & C Black guide for writers of all sorts, the *Writers' and Artists' Yearbook*, used to dismiss "Markets for Verse" in a page and a half. They could have done it in one line — there are none. In commercial terms it is a hopeless case. Save your energy, think up slogans for chocolate-bar competitions, stand on your head.

This book began in the 1970s as a pamphlet for the Association of Little Presses. It was written in response to pleas from editors and press operators up and down the country who were awash with manuscripts: poems everywhere, most of them lousy, an awful lot submitted badly, to the wrong places, the wrong way, without return postage, without a contact address. What had happened was that for the first time in history it had become more popular to write poetry than to read it. The flood was flowing and it hasn't turned yet. Michael Anania, former president of America's Co-ordinating Council of Literary Magazines, noted "editorial offices of established magazines drifted over with manuscripts, and new magazines born to meet the writer's need for print. Increasingly," he continued, "magazines seem to reflect a sociological circumstance as much as an aesthetic one." Literary movements and schools of poetry are no longer all-commanding. The poets, by simply existing, create the need for publication. Because they demand it, new magazines begin. There should be no shortage — if you can write you'll find a way in.

This sounds like success, yet it isn't. Ultimately poetry periodicals do not sell. There are hundreds of them, certainly, but their circulations are almost always small. Most sell between 200 and a thousand copies each issue; only a very few claim to do better. If you broke down sales of a typical 300-circulation poetry magazine it would look like this:

Contributors' copies	35
File copies	6
Copyright copies	6
Complimentary and review copies	40
Library subscriptions (which often go unread)	30
Damaged and unsold copies	80
Copies actually sold	103

All that publishing effort for 103 people? And how many of those bought one just to keep the editor happy, to make him stop pestering them and go away? But let's get this in proportion:

Population of the UK	55,000,000
Viewers of *Neighbours*	12,000,000
Purchasers of *The Sun*	4,000,000
Readers of *The Guardian*	450,000
Readers of a typical poetry magazine	103

Is that it then?

> Little poetry magazines have always functioned primarily for writers. Readers are desirable, sometimes even actively sought out, but the impulse behind most magazines is the writer/editor's conviction that there are writers who are not being served by existing publications.
>
> Michael Anania

You might feel inclined now to throw your poems in the bin and have done with it. Yet you can improve things; there *is* an audience, a large one, reluctant but tappable — the poets, the people doing this versifying, even you. You can buy books, you can read magazines. In fact if you've any inclination at all to write and publish contemporary poetry you must do this. Appendix 1 lists a number of specialist poetry bookshops. Contact them to find out what is available; buy — convince your local bookshop that there is a demand and ask them to expand the tiny poetry section they already have.

Poetry has a widespread but very thin market — invisible when viewed for profit — but it's there. If you want your poems bought and read, then most likely it is going to be by people similar to yourself. They'll treat poetry as you do. Improve things, buy books yourself. Start now.

2
Why Write?

Poetry is indispensable! If only I knew what for.
Jean Cocteau

This non-stop flood of creative writing must have a reason. Why are half the population writing, a "sullen art" as Dylan Thomas put it, when instead they could be making pots, growing flowers or talking to their friends? Writing is hardly a relaxation. Probably the majority of all authors dislike the process and can only relax when they've done. *PN Review* editor Michael Schmidt blames the system — education, he says, encourages writing at the expense of reading. Self-expression, what's inside you has to come out. People hardly write letters any more, there is no need. They do not keep journals or diaries. They make cassette recordings and take self- focusing snaps. When they write, they do so to articulate emotion, to fix and name what they feel, to create in undemanding blobs and then move on. It's how they've seen it done. No rules. Almost anything goes. Poetry — the work arrives by sleight of hand. It is apt, high art yet manageable; there is exultation in engaging in it; it does not go on for too long. Poetry is easy, all beginners think so.

But of course they are wrong.

Many thousands of novice poets in this country suffer this grand delusion. They think that once they've actually written something this act alone makes them important. They imagine it turns them overnight into vital creators with something to say. Poetry is at first a matter of apprenticeship and hard work. They ignore this. They insist that what they've scribbled is enough, they want it published. I just cannot imagine similar people buying a violin, scratching a few notes and then applying to join the London Symphony Orchestra. Ah, but poetry is different — yes: it does different things.

Ken Edwards of the magazine *Reality Studios*:

90 per cent of people writing poetry in this country *don't read it*. Poetry is an outlet for people who feel depressed, undervalued, ignored, marginal. It appears to be an easy route to fame, success, recognition and doesn't involve boring things like learning how to play a musical instrument or getting access to equipment. Unfortunately, this is not so.

12

Many people suffering this desire to write could not sustain a novel or comparable long work in the time they have available. Their day is fragmented by other demands — job, children, food, house, tiredness, TV — the poem is the perfect vehicle: they can put it together in as brief a time as a couple of hours. I don't think there is anything wrong with this. I don't believe that only special sorts of people are able to write. "Being creative, *making*, is a fundamental human condition," says Nigel Jenkins.

It should be possible for most people to write some kind of poetry. The problem, as I've pointed out, lies in the overpowering hunger to rush into print. Hold back, perfect what you do before you insist on showing it around.

I suppose, actually, the fact that you want to *publish* what you've written is a good sign. Much poetry gets written for personal reasons — exorcizing emotions, depleting desperations, dealing with love and coping with despair. This kind of writing is therapeutic and should be left in the drawer. If you feel what you've written goes beyond that, then persevere. There may be something worth printing from you yet.

In the research for this book I spent some time asking poets — experienced and inexperienced alike — why they wrote. Most, in their off-the-cuff answers, said that they didn't know. When later I sent a questionnaire and asked for written replies, things had changed. Given time, justifications had been found:

Edwin Morgan: "It is an urge."

C.H. Sisson: "It is a disease."

Ivor Cutler: "To get attention, for excitement."

Tony Conran: "To show off, to entertain. I run away from writing poetry, as a general rule, until it corners me."

Some still couldn't really say though:

Fleur Adcock: "When it happens, I can't help it."

Liliane Lijn: "I don't *try* to write poetry. But there are times when I have to say something . . ."

Quoted more than once was Charles Olson's description of a poem as "energy transferred from where the poet got it. . .by way of the poem as itself. . .to the reader." But this still avoided the why.

Raymond Garlick came nearer: "It was sparked off by a kind of irritation. Ceasing to write some 35 years later, seemed to coincide with an awareness that most of the causes of tension in one's life had evaporated or become much modified." Poetry, an instigator, an articulator of change. Finally Irish poet James Simmons produced what was for me the most acceptable reason: "At first because poets had helped me to make sense of the world and myself. I wanted to be a part of what they did. It gradually became a way of life . . ." Only then, once it's a way of life, can the poetry develop. So it doesn't matter that you do not know why you write poetry, only that you do.

Poetry is one of the most efficient techniques that there is of self-examination and of contemplating the world.

Peter Redgrove and Penelope Shuttle

The poet is primarily concerned not with communicating information but with making things happen; he aims not at talking about the emotion that is the starting point of his poem, but at causing that emotion to be reflected in the sensibility of his reader.

Vernon Scannell

But it doesn't matter really if you are totally unaware of all this. Just write.

When I began composing poems in the early 1960s I started, I think, because I admired the lifestyle. I had no real *literary* pretensions at that time, yet the idea of being somehow part of an alternative society, as I imagined all poets to be, appealed. Poets lived in garrets, didn't they? They were Bohemians, Beats, Angry Young Men. My first poetry-reading disillusioned me. Six Welsh poets, all of them middle-aged, all of them wearing suits. Even the late John Tripp, *enfant terrible* of Cardiff literary society, hadn't let them down. He wore a roll-neck sweater and had combed his hair. The evening was formal and it was boring. It took me a while to find out that readings didn't have to be like this.

Images rarely conform to reality. During Vernon Scannell's period as a kind of resident village poet at Berinsfield in Oxfordshire, a local was asked if Mr Scannell was her idea of a poet. No, she replied, "Poets are dirty, and they've got beards and they wear scruffy clothes." The Bohemian image, despite a changed society, persists. When a group of schoolchildren were asked to give their descriptions of a poet the results were surprisingly consistent:

"A boring old man, scruffy, weak."

"An uninteresting person who stays in his room and writes about things he's never done."

"A miserable, middle-aged person who is bald and reads a lot."

"A lonely old man with a harsh voice, and lots of pencils and scribbled-on papers all around his desk."

"A soft, elderly sort. Always mumbling into his beard." All old, you'll notice, and none of them women.

Poets are actually as varied as bus queues — the only thing that unites them is that they all follow the creative impulse, they all write.

This book is not a primer in poetics but it is always interesting for the beginner to study the work-practices of others. *Writers at Work — The Paris Review Interviews* — collected in seven volumes and now available in paperback — are a good source. A wide range of writers are included — novelists, dramatists and many poets — all inveigled into leaking the tricks of their trade. The important thing they seem to say is to persist: pursue the idea; don't give up. Carry notebooks. Always remember that if you don't record an idea at the moment it arrives intervening time will change it, or more likely when eventually you try to write it down you'll have forgotten what it was.

> If not used at once, all may vanish as a dream; worse, future creation may be endangered — for only the removal and development of the material frees the (creative) forces for further work.
>
> Tillie Olsen

- *Think.*
- *Read.*
- *Write.*

And if you are certain that poetry is more important to you than simply a romantic attachment to the idea of "being a bit of a writer" — then keep on.

3
How Good Is It?

. . .as for literature
it gives no man a sinecure.

And no one knows, at sight, a masterpiece.
And give up verse, my boy,
There's nothing in it.

Ezra Pound

How good am I? This is the question most asked by the new poet
— Am I writing poetry at all? Edison said talent was 1 per cent
inspiration and 99 per cent perspiration. He was referring to talent
for invention but for poetry it's the same. You've sweated — what
you want now is someone to approve, to tell you it's worth going
on. "Am I a poet?" a novice once asked C. Day Lewis. "You cannot
be," was the reply, "or you would not have enquired." There is
a lot in this — ultimately what you decide to call yourself or to think
of yourself as is up to you. But it is quite natural early on to want
some confirmation that you are not wasting your time. You need
criticism, an appraisal of what you are doing, but BEWARE:

- The remarks of friends and relations should not invariably be
  trusted. Their criticisms are not dispassionate — they are people
  who do not want to see you hurt and are likely therefore to bend
  the truth. It may be also that they know little of poetry and will
  base their remarks entirely on benevolence. This may be pleasing
  but it won't do you any good. How many editors have read letters
  which begin: "I enclose a collection of my poetry for your
  consideration. My friends tell me that it is very good." Usually
  it is not.
- Your own desire for criticism is not entirely impartial. Rigorous,
  honest evaluation can be hurtful. Do you really want that? Or
  are you just after praise?
- Critical judgements based on your early work can themselves be
  valueless. Herman Hesse in his *Letter to a Young Poet* remarks
  that a new writer would have to be "actually lacking in normal
  endowment if he were not able to write acceptable poems", and

16

then shows as an example the early work of Goethe where it is difficult to discern any particular talent at all.

Yet some kind of informed comment on what you've done so far is bound to be of use. Where can you get it?

1: *From other writers.* You could post your work to them with a covering letter asking for an opinion. But do not expect a lot, a professional writer's time is valuable. History is littered with cases of novice poets nurtured by the famous. It will surely be your luck, however, to receive a printed postcard informing you that the author is unable to comment as you request.

2: *From poets at readings.* Catch them before they go. They are highly likely to glance at your work briefly while you watch and then mumble appreciatively. They won't wish to offend. Treat what they tell you with care.

3: *From criticism sessions at writers' workshops* — perhaps the best and cheapest method. Such groups often meet to discuss members' work, and although there is a tendency to skate around difficulties and avoid confrontation the experience should be had. See Chapter 18 for fuller details.

4: *From critical services* — a number of these schemes are run by the Regional Arts Associations and usually consist of a panel of experts — critics, editors, poets, novelists — who in exchange for a fee will read new work and provide a report on it. See Appendix 2 for a list of the Regional Arts Associations. If there is not such a scheme in your area — and coverage is patchy — you could approach the Poetry Society at 21 Earl's Court Square, London SW5. Their service, founded by Norman Hidden, is based on an appraisal of 200 lines of work within which length, they say, a poet's major strengths and weaknesses are usually apparent. A written report is prepared following a close reading of the text and the poet is told where he or she is going right or wrong. The Society stresses two things: that their critics are only able to tell poets the truth *as they see it*, and that the scheme itself is designed for those "attempting to take a professional attitude towards their work for the first time". The cost at 1991 prices is £23.00, with reductions for Society members. Some privately run schemes are also available and you'll find them advertised in the writers' magazines. For poets, though, they tend to be a little expensive.

It is also possible to get an idea of how you are doing by actually sending your work out for publication; but more of that in Chapter 5.

With its reference to "professional attitude", the Poetry Society implies the existence of both professional and amateur poets. Of course nobody actually makes a living from poetry, but you can get by by working in allied fields — teaching poetry, writing about poetry, reviewing poetry, giving poetry readings, talking occasionally on television and more frequently on the radio about verse. Another paradox: you can earn more from dealing in poetry than you can from writing the stuff itself. The Scottish Arts Council loosely defines the professional poet as "someone whose work can command a fee and who has a track record of publication; in other words, someone who can demonstrate professional status." Is this for you? Where do you want to fit in?

The late Howard Sergeant, founder of *Outposts*, one of the longest running of British magazines — still continuing under the editorship of Roland John — divided the field into three main groups:

— First, what he called the "Establishment mafia", where the poets are a small powerful group, devolved from the universities. They know each other, review each other's books, are all editors of something — a magazine, a publishing house, a radio programme. Their names revolve on an "inner wheel", turning up in most of poetry's outlets again and again. This group, numbering around a dozen and a half, does occasoinally change but so rarely that it has led outsiders to believe that you have to be the literary equivalent of a mason to get in.

— Secondly, the individualists who keep going "despite the Establishment, breaking through entirely on the quality of their work" or have enough energy to start outlets — magazines, publishing houses — of their own.

— Thirdly, Sergeant identified what he regarded as potentially the most important group — "a mass of people writing their poems in a vacuum, who know little about the literary world and its workings, nothing of the Establishment, yet who continue to write their poems because they have to." Howard Sergeant may have over- simplified, but in essence he's probably right.

It is worth mentioning here the special position of the woman writer. For most of printing history the annual proportion of published works written by women has been as low as 20 per cent. This is not for actual lack of female writers but for reasons of culture and society and the hierarchy of control. This figure has been consistent from 1800 to well into the 1960s and has only very recently begun to rise. When critical reaction is analysed over a similar period, the percentage favourable to work by women is a mere 8 per cent. Peter Redgrove believes that it is the male definition of Great Poetry which is at fault: "It is only something that specially inspired great people, usually men, can produce." For women different criteria ought to apply. And how many female poetry editors are there? Not enough — but there is change in the wind.

Which brings me to the vexed question of exactly who these people are? Who is it who sits in judgement on what you write? How did these selectors, editors and publishers get their appointments? Often as members of Howard Sergeant's "Establishment mafia" they appear to be born into office; yet many are ordinary creative individuals drawn to the posts they fill by a combination of interest and accident. They are involved because they want to be. I once saw a panel of distinguished literati at Poetry Day at the London School of Economics berated for having passed no "editor's exams", whatever they are.

Judgement exercised by a poetry editor comes from experience, writing poetry, reading poetry, and of course in actually having to make selections from other people's verse.

Go to it. Take the poems out of the drawer and read them again. If they still seem worthy, it might be time to try sending them off.

4
Publication — Preparation of Manuscripts

Most authors would consider it undesirable to approach a publisher
in a dirty and incoherent condition. But that is, in effect, what
they do when they submit a dirty and dilapidated manuscript.
Sir Stanley Unwin

Publication — which is the central theme of this book — can actually
mean a number of things. To publish, according to *Chambers'
Twentieth-Century Dictionary* is "to make public, to divulge, to
announce, to proclaim". This can be accomplished in many ways:
you can stand on a street corner and recite your verses, you can sing
them, or you can read them out loud at a public gathering, say a
creative writing class — and for many poets this *is* their first
publication, a way of showing others what they've written and of
obtaining a reaction in return. Others have photocopied single poems
and distributed them *samizdat* fashion, or been lucky enough to have
their work broadcast on radio. Publication can mean tape-recording,
film, microfiche, or even the inclusion of verse in an information-
retrieval system such as teletext, or as data manipulated by the
program of a computer. Telephone poems are possible — you can
leave them on an answering machine. You may wish to carve a poem
in stone, as Ian Hamilton Finlay has done, and install it as sculpture
in your garden, or do as the medieval Japanese and paint your *haiku*
on to hillside rocks. The contemporary equivalent of this is verse
graffitied via spray-can on to walls and doors.

But for most of us publication means print — poetry set in type
and reproduced on paper. Print implies merit, truth; it imparts status.
If you've a poem *printed*, everyone can recognize your achievement,
even if they know nothing of verse. Years of propaganda, advertising,
newspaper reportage and all the other half-truths and untruths of
the published word have failed to take their toll. The feeling that
print equals respectability persists. It cannot be devalued — printed
publication is for most of us a yardstick with which to measure
success.

You should at this stage have a clear understanding of the

difference between printer and publisher. Printers own and operate the equipment which actually reproduces the work. Publishers are entrepreneurial middlemen: they buy texts from authors, pay printers to turn them into books and then market the product through booksellers. The confusion arises when some printers also turn out to be publishers, some publishers operate their own printing equipment and others call themselves *presses* when they actually own no such equipment at all. As a general rule, however, take it that publishers publish and printers print.

Presentation

If you want your poems turned into print, first you have to type them. Some new poets baulk at this — "I can't type, I haven't a machine, it's what I've written that is important, not how it looks. My handwriting is neat enough." Typewriters are now quite old-fashioned instruments and in the world of publishing they have universal acceptability. If you submit handwritten work it will appear to most as rankly amateur and in all likelihood will not be given a second glance.

Buy a typewriter — they are not inordinately expensive and you can get some fine reconditioned office models second-hand. It's worth noting that cheap portables won't stand constant pounding, so if you are prolific invest in one that costs a little more. Don't waste your money at this stage on an expensive daisywheel electric model. They may produce brilliant-looking copy but when they go wrong — and this is inevitable with complex machines — they cost a lot to repair. (I knew a man once who spent hundreds on an electric varispace typer with a view to making his work exude professionalism. The machine jammed after a few weeks and no matter what he did he couldn't put it right. There were no engineers locally, no repair shops and in the end, completely frustrated and powerless, he lost his temper and hit it with a hammer. I think he turned to painting after that.) Word processors are the ultimate answer, if you can afford one and are willing to learn how to use it. No doubt they are more benefit to the prose-writer but poets will still find them amazingly time saving. Gone are the endlessly crossed-out and altered verses, the bin overflowing with crumpled paper; changes are now made directly onto a screen. When you are happy with the result you print it out. From the humble Amstrad priced now at under £300 to an Applemac which can set you back a few thousands the possibilities are there for poets to produce versions of their work which look better than those in anthologies on library shelves.

It is always possible to use a typing agency, of course, but these cost money. If your reason for sticking to handwriting is that you can't type then you ought to learn. For a poet, two-finger typing, self-taught, will suffice. I've never taken a typing lesson in my life and do all the wrong things like looking at the keyboard and using only half a hand, yet I can still type faster than I can write. Many poets find the discipline of typing as they compose useful; others regard typewriters and word-processors as anathema and will only use them to produce final drafts. There is even a branch of writing exclusive to the machines — typewriter poetry — which makes art of the keyboard's parameters and the style of its letters. See *Typewriter Poems* (Second Aeon/Something Else Press) if you'd like to learn more.

In the publishing world a typed poem is called perversely a *manuscript* (MS for short), although I have noticed a move recently to call it a *typescript* (TS for short), which makes more sense. The accepted form for a MS is as follows:

1. Type the poem *exactly* as you would wish it to appear in print. No double spacings unless actually required. *Underline* words which are to appear in an italic typeface. Use a black ribbon, as this reproduces best if a photocopy is made.

2. Position the poem centrally on a white sheet of A4 paper, leaving as wide a margin *all round* as you can.

3. If the poem is longer than a single page (i.e. more than 50 lines) finish it on a continuation sheet, indicating at the bottom of page 1 and the top of page 2 that this is what you have done. To avoid printers putting a space you might not want into your poem, write in the bottom right-hand corner something similar to "poem continues, no line break", or "poem continues, after break of one line". Type a page number on each sheet and staple the group in the top left-hand corner.

4. Every poem should have a title. That sounds obvious but it is amazing the number that do not. A title is a handle — a poetry editor will use it while considering the work. If you don't have one (and you may have artistic reasons for this), the poem

will become known by its first line, or else be detailed in contents pages as *untitled*, and that can miss your point. A title will also prevent an editor from mistaking a new poem for the second part of a longer poem. If you really can't think of anything, call it *Poem* — which is better than nothing, but only just.

5. As you type, check your spellings and any grammar you may be doubtful of. *Fowler's Modern English Usage*, revised by Sir Ernest Gowers (Oxford University Press), is the best guide.

6. If the poem suddenly starts sounding odd — stop. Take it out of the typewriter and read it again. You may have to rewrite. If there is any doubt, hold back.

7. Put your name at the end of the poem, and, *most important*, your address. Do not assume that because you are typing up a batch of work you don't have to do this on every piece — poems can become detached.

8. Do not clutter the MS with references like "First British serial rights offered", or "320 words". In the case of poetry such appendages don't mean a thing.

9. Make a copy as you type, renewing your carbon as often as you can. It is best to use black and if the copy comes out smudged to throw it away and start again. Photocopies of MSS — if you have access to a machine — are perfectly acceptable and are in many ways better than carbons since they don't smear.

10. Whatever happens, ALWAYS KEEP A FILE COPY FOR YOURSELF — top, carbon or photo. Don't ever send or lend this out. Keep it in the house.

11. When you've finished, read your typed copy through again. If you find an error, correct it as cleanly as possible. You can't go round and explain to the editor how meticulous you actually are about your work and that the smudges and corrections all over it don't really reflect any compositional sloppiness — the MS itself must do that.

Don't stop now. The next stage is sending it in.

5
Sending It In

Your first attempts at publication — getting a poem "accepted" — should be directed at magazines. Start where you'll have the best chance and then move on. Anthologies, if you were considering these as an alternative, are usually selected from poems which have previously appeared elsewhere. A publisher dealing in collections of poems by individual authors will want to see what else you've done. In any event, "For the first 10 to 15 years," as Raymond Garlick advises, "try to control any obsession about getting a book out: it's likely to be a millstone round your neck later on." Ten years may be slightly on the long side but the advice is sound. Magazines are where to start. Initially you'll need to find out what and where they are; see Chapter 6 on markets. Study this closely before you begin.

You'll have to do the sending in yourself too. Literary agents (listed in both *The Writers' Handbook* (Macmillan) and *The Writers' and Artists' Yearbook* (A & C Black) for the determined) rarely touch poetry, and if one does it is usually from a represented author successful in other fields, such as a novelist perhaps. I did hear of one poet safeguarding himself against the pains of rejection by getting his wife to do all the submitting for him. She was only to mention the subject if they'd had any luck. Life was all silence or success — he never ever heard at first hand any of his work actually being sent back. If you have the opportunity to do this, don't take it. The experience of rejection is as important as that of success.

When you are submitting your work the following points should all be borne in mind:

● *Research your market*. Do not simply send your work to the first apparently suitable address you find. Read widely, actually support the magazines you've picked. Be perfectly clear of the kind of thing they print and assure yourself that you will fit in.

● *Keep a record book*. List the name and address of magazine, date of submission, titles of poems sent and then leave a space where you can record reaction.

● *Send around 6 poems at a time* — short to medium length if you've got them and avoiding epics. Show a range of subject matter and style. Give the editor as much variety as possible to increase your chance of acceptance.

- *Do not go overboard.* In no circumstances submit your life's work. There is nothing more likely to put an editor off than a bulky parcel enmeshed with rubber bands and string accompanied by a letter beginning: "I enclose 300 poems written over the past few months . . ."

- *Should you send the same poem to more than one place simultaneously?* This is a matter for disagreement. In some ways it is not ethical to offer work as unpublished when it could actually be on the point of acceptance elsewhere. On the other hand you may think it unreasonable to tie up a poem which may have taken a long time to write by submitting it to a magazine which could hold it under consideration for many months and then subsequently send it back. You might also like to consider what kind of exclusivity can be demanded by a magazine with a circulation of 500 or less which pays nothing more than a free copy for the work it uses. It is up to you, but take care. If you get a reputation for publishing the same poem in a variety of places you could find everything being turned down, good or not. At very least, if you decide on dual submission, advise other editors who may be considering your poem as soon as you learn of its acceptance elsewhere.

- *A brief accompanying letter* will act as a bridge between you and the editor. Find out the appropriate editor's name if you can and use it. Don't be too impersonal. Don't include irrelevant information. Don't try to justify your poetry; the MS itself should do that. Some poets, especially Americans, include a full curriculum vitae, giving achievements, education, marital status and all kinds of other information, which I think overdoes it somewhat. Be careful about acknowledging previous publication if you have any. Great lists of obscure little magazines should be avoided and especially do not mention any dealings you might have had with the vanity press (see Chapter 15). The aim of a c.v. is to boost you — the fact that you've been published in a range of odd-sounding, low-circulation journals will be of no great support when, for example, attempting to place your work with a larger-circulation national literary review. In my book of short stories *Between 35 and 42* I included a fictitious and very lengthy list of small mags in which I claimed previous publication.

Running out of actual names, I padded the list out with the names of plants. *Rodgersia Pinnata*, I wrote, *Myrobalan*, *Privet*, *Edith Nellie Perkins*. And it was amazing the number of people who failed to see the joke — "Who edits this *Waterside Dogwood* then?" they would say. If you have won literary prizes or awards, mention them. Swimming certificates or ability at darts are out. I'd ignore the photo, too. Its inclusion is a practice of the middle-aged and otherwise faded, who generally enclose one of themselves beaming-faced, taken when they were young. Simple information is the rule. Try not to brag.

Some things you shouldn't do:

- *Don't bribe*. Don't offer to subscribe *if* your poems are accepted (an editor would like you to subscribe anyway). Don't say you'll buy dozens of copies of the issue you're in to sell to your friends. Don't mention how much bad luck you've had, how long you've been hunting for publication, your lack of success. Don't plead, suggest how desperate, depressed or deranged you are. Don't mention last hopes, lost hopes or in fact any kind of hope at all. Don't explain why you've chosen his magazine, don't praise it falsely, don't be overly deferential. Don't mention suicide, or how you must succeed this time to prove yourself. Don't spend more time fussing about submission to magazines than you actually do writing. That's far more important than sending in. Rewrite it six times, submit it once.

- *Enclose a stamped addressed envelope* large enough to accommodate your submission and with enough stamps on it to pay for their weight. THIS IS VITAL. If you don't pay in advance for the return of your MSS it is unlikely that you'll see them again. To be deplored is the practice of unaccompanied photocopies with a note to the effect that they should be thrown away if not wanted and the poet only contacted in the event of acceptance. Do not submit your poems in overly large envelopes, fancy packaging or by registered or recorded mail. To you the poems may be of unique importance — to the editor they are just another batch. Be like everyone else, use standard 220 x 110 mm or 250 x 180 mm, brown manila, second-class mail.

- *After you've mailed your envelope, expect to wait*. You may hear after a few days, but usually it takes weeks. There is no hard-and-fast rule — surveyed magazines quote "report times" (the gap between receiving a submission and sending a reply) varying between two weeks and three months. A lot will depend on the time of year, if the editor is on holiday, or if an issue has just been published which means the editor will be in the middle of a lot of extra work. In my experience, three weeks is about average. There are some magazines, however, who don't reply at all until they are just about to go to press, at which stage they send back everything which is not required. The rule is patience, hold on.

● *Finally, don't complain.* Your poems may be new and vital, and it is certainly unreasonable for some editor to keep them dark and unread for month after month, but *you* chose to submit them. *The editor didn't ask.* It will do you no good writing, it will be embarrassing if you phone and in no circumstances whatsoever turn up in person to find out what's going on. In my days as editor of *Second Aeon* I had all of these things happen and I can't recall any of the poems complained about being any good. If six months pass and you hear nothing, enquire by postcard but leave it at that.

The information I've left out so far concerns what happens when you get a result. How are you told? No fanfares, it slides in via a brief letter, sometimes on a reversed rejection slip attached to the returned part of your originally submitted batch. There is nothing too formal about it — editors may be renowned for sending curt rejection slips but they mail brief acceptances too.

Most editors would agree that poetry attracts eccentrics. Potential contributors ring up and dicatate verse down the phone; turn up and sing it to you; recite the latest in your ear loudly, when they catch you having a quiet drink in the pub. Enormous scripts arrive by all posts — poetry in use for every conceivable end. I used to be irritated by the overly religious and the dogmatically political — always long — inevitably sent without stamps. Poetry mags are usually run by one individual who is not a public service, no matter where he might apply to get his funds.

For me the post always arrived early — great wodges of it banging into the hall, fat brown envelopes sliding around like fish. I'd open a few straight away, take those I fancied back to bed to read and leave the rest until later. Don't ask me how I decided — it certainly wasn't on names — it was completely arbitrary, influenced by whim.

A great many potential poetry mag contributors imagine editors to lead a free, wild and Bohemian life. The literary scene is replete with tales of visiting poets arriving unannounced, drunk, bearing wine. The editors are somehow always found asleep, sober and pretty keen on the status quo. It is best, I think, to approach poetry magazines with, if not respect, at least consideration.

Poetry may be different, its practitioners attuned to a wider spectrum, yet it is no vehicle for gratuitous eccentricty. Play it straight; that way you'll stand a better chance.

6
Markets — the Individual Poem

Where do you send it? The previous chapter talked about beginning with magazines, but do you know what these are? Where do you see poetry used? For most of the public poetry is an irrelevancy. They ignore it. They imagine, I suppose, that it isn't there. But if you look hard you'll find it and the longer you look the more you'll see.

At the popular end — light verse, humorous rhyme, easy sentiment — you can actually make money out of it. If this is you —good luck. Outlets include:

— Greetings cards.

— Letters written in rhyming doggerel to the editors of popular papers and magazines.

— Hearts and flowers styled moralizing and sentimentality — again doggerel. Often verse compressed as prose to save space used by some women's magazines.

Most poets, however, have a more serious intent. Here are some places which could be tried:

Quality newspapers

The Times, *Guardian*, *Daily Telegraph*, etc., all occasionally print poetry. More frequent use is made by the Sundays — *The Observer*, *Sunday Times*, *Sunday Telegraph*. But it is usually one short poem per issue, and almost inevitably the known poets who appear.

Quality weeklies

The Listener, *The Literary Review*, *New Statesman and Society*, *London Review of Books*, and *The Spectator*, etc. — much like the newspapers although the lesser-known poet stands a slightly better chance.

Women's magazines

She, *The Lady*, *Woman and Home*, *Spare Rib*, etc. This very slim market is dominated by reprints of popular poems and work from the established, although occasionally the odd newcomer can break in.

Specialist periodicals

Magazines devoted to fishing, homemaking, brewing, planes, ships, model railways, African affairs, the church and so forth generally do not seek poetry, but if you have something written in their subject area do try sending it in. Much can be done by personal initiative; write to the editor and suggest the establishment of a poetry page, even offer to edit it. Such proposals — particularly with country and county journals — have actually been known to work.

Events and review periodicals

Time Out, *City Limits*, *Venue*, *What's Happening*, etc., where arts and entertainments are listed and discussed. These sometimes print work from poets living in their area, although usually it is in conjunction with a book publication or other literary event.

Radio and television

A thin market, but Radios 3 and 4 do use verse in some of their programmes. Here is the entry from *Writing for the BBC*:

> In addition to anthologies and critical programmes which feature or discuss published poetry, both classical and contemporary, there are two series, both on Radio 3, which are devoted to recent work. *The Living Poet*, an occasional series, is confined to the work of one poet selected on the initiative of the producer. *Poetry Now*, broadcast once a month at a duration of twenty minutes, is made up of readings of unpublished verse. Material for this programme should be sent to the Editor, *Poetry Now*, Broadcasting House, London. Radio 4 broadcasts regular poetry series, but these offer no outlet for unpublished work by living writers.

TV stations have also been known to broadcast a poem at closedown occasionally and local radio often has an arts slot which either does or can be cajoled into featuring verse. If payment doesn't concern you and you've an extrovert side to your nature this could be an area worth pushing.

Crafts

A highly personalized area where certain poets have successfully co-operated with artists and craftspeople in the production of calendars, postcards, tea-towels, posters, prints, even tie-pins, rings and ceramic work. To become involved you would need to know people working in such media and be sympathetic to their aims.

Recordings

Spoken word and audio book recordings are produced by many companies, although almost always of established poets. Some arts associations, however, have made tapes of regional verse but the market is small and usually solicited.

Dial-a-poem

These telephone services operate like British Telecom's Dial-a-disc, Bedtime Story and the Speaking Clock, but are run by local arts bodies like the Regional Arts Associaitons. Britain's most successful service was run by the Welsh Arts Council in the early 1970s and received hundreds of thousands of calls.

Vanity press anthologies

Typical titles are: *Best Poems of 1991*, *Diadem of the Muse*, and so forth. You contribute by responding to small ads requesting verse which appear in the classified sections of newspapers. There is a charge for publication, and the results if you do pay are always completely worthless. AVOID SUCH ENTERPRISES AT ALL COSTS (see Chapter 15).

Literary magazines

As you will have read in Chapter 5, this is the biggest market of all. Literary periodicals can be divided roughly into two:

(a) *The larger-circulation, review-based, discursive magazines* which include poetry as part of their editorial policy. A number of these periodicals are heavily subsidised. They include *Encounter*, *The Literary Review*, *London Magazine*, *The Times Literary Supplement*, *Critical Quarterly* and so on. National distribution is standard and all would continue to function quite normally if they were never sent another poem. New work from new writers is included but not much and competition is fierce.

(b) *The little magazine* — the major outlet for poetry in Britain and Ireland. They've been around a long time. In the nineteenth century, *Cornhill* and *Bentley's Miscellany*; in the early twentieth, *Blast*, *The Egoist*, *The English Review* — important purveyors of emerging modernism. By 1947 Hoffman, Allen and Ulrich note in their survey *The Little Magazine* that the " little reviews" had become the prime outlet for 80 per cent of our most important poets. Into the 1990s this percentage remains unchanged.

What distinguishes a little mag is not its physical size but its origin. It is not the product of big companies and large organizations. The little mag is the prerogative of the individudual — often complete one-person operations from editing to selling on the street. They range from photocopied journals set on a portable typewriter to bulky spine-bound publications that look much more like books than magazines. There is as much range in their content. Magazines exist devoted to specific schools, styles, groups, biases, theories, verse forms, interests, districts, countries, occupations, political colourings and racial background. *All* forms have their outlet.

Elliott Anderson and Mary Kinzie in their *The Little Magazine in America* suggest that contributors are "people writing against the grain. . .who nevertheless want recognition. Not content to wait until the new sensibility of which they may be the harbingers has proven itself in time, they insist on a revolution in taste now." Although this is only part of the picture — countless magazines exist to maintain the status quo — it does indicate why the little mags are so vital to the literary arts. They are proving grounds for new styles and new voices. Because of their economic organization they are able to take risks — able, in fact, to cavort in utter abandonment of all convention if they so wish, and of course some do. Collectively, they are a combination of avant-garde laboratory and social service. Within them, all reasonably accomplished poetry can find a home.

According to S.T. Gardiner, in a survey he carried out for *Poets Yearbook*, the average little mag has five issues in two years and a circulation of 500 copies. He further calculates that their total sale — and I estimate there to be around 200 British little mags — accounts for half the poetry sold in the UK. There is always talk of a boom in poetry as well; any day now someone will make their living from it. It's rumour, of course. And until the mass-market paperbackers find it rewarding enough to put poetry on station bookstalls, so it will remain.

Among the hundreds of British little mags, many with colourful names, there is a distinct pecking-order. It is difficult to quantify because it changes, often from month to month, as fortunes shift, new magazines start and old ones fail. From Denys Val Baker's survey of dozens of forties little mags only two are publishing today: *Poetry Review* and *Outposts*.

At the top are the larger, better-heeled operations which usually purport to reflect the state of poetry as it is today. Their success in achieving this aim varies considerably. They include both the aforementioned champions of longevity *Poetry Review* and *Outposts* along with *PN Review*, *Agenda*, *Ambit* and *Stand*. It is a sextet which has remained unchanged for many years.

Below lie periodicals which restrict their contents to work from a specific region –– *Poetry Durham*, *The Honest Ulsterman*, *The New Welsh Review*, *Poetry Ireland Review*, *The North*, *Poetry Wales*, *Edinburgh Review*, *Chester Poets* or to work of a specific kind — for example *Fragmente* which concentrates on contemporary poetics, *Krax* for humorous verse and *Psychopoetica* which has an interst in psychologically based work. There are also magazines such as *First Time* which only uses previously unpublished writers and *Tears In The Fence* which promotes environmental concerns.

The vast bulk of magazines know no specific allegiance beyond the interest of their editors. Some are solid and regular like *Orbis*, others — *A Doctor's Dilemma*, *Strength Beyond Bingo*, or *Kite* seem to move with the wind. The list is enormous: *And*, *Aquarius*, *Chapman*, *Global Tapestry Journal*, *Iron*, *Lobby Press Newsletter*, *Kroklok*, *Poetry Olympics*, *Tenth Decade*, *Oasis*, *Slow Dancer*, *Spectacular Diseases*, *Weyfarers*, *Iota*, *Joe Soap's Canoe*, *Poet's Voice*, *Verse*, *Pennine Platform*, *Ore*, *Bogg*, *The Echo Room*, *X-Calibre*, *Krino*, *Label*, *Mar*, *Momentum*, *New Prospects*, *Numbers*,

Otter, *Pen:Umbra*, *Planet*, *The Printer's Devil*, *Rhinoceros*, *The Rialto*, *The Salmon*, *Spokes*, *The Whiterose Literary Magazine*, *The Wide Skirt*, *The Works* — the list goes on and on.

Little mags are small. Don't expect to get treated as you would be by a larger concern. Not all are exclusively poetry either — many deal in criticism or fiction or both. Find out what they do before you send off your work.

Editors often complain that publicity brings a great increase in potential contributions to their pages but very few subscribers. People want to be published, they don't want to read. As a consequence the magazines often sell so poorly that publication in some of them becomes a dubious honour. Buy, subscribe first, send in later on.

Locating your market

Unfortunately there is no one comprehensive address sourcebook for all UK poetry markets. Many have been tried but the scene changes so frequently and so quickly that as soon as a list is compiled it goes out of date. You may, however, like to consult the following:

- *The Writer's Handbook* edited by Barry Turner (Macmillan) and *The Writers' and Artists' Yearbook* (A & C Black) — available from booksellers, both currently £7.95. Both of these complete reference books for the writer have sections of specialist information for the poet. Both list "commercial" magazine and newspaper publishers with *The Writer's Handbook* going on to cover a large number of small magazines.

- *PALPI* — *Poetry and Little Press Information* (Association of Little Presses, 89a Petherton Road, London N5 2QT — available on subscription, £4.50) lists, three times a year, recent little mags and small presses together with other information.

- Either *Poet's Market* compiled annually by Judson Jerome for Writer's Digest Books (available in the UK at £15.25 from Freelance Press Services, 5/9 Bexley Sq, Salford, Manchester M3 6DB) or Len Fulton and Ellen Ferber's *Directory of Poetry Publishers* (priced at approx £12.00 direct from Dustbooks, PO Box 100, Paradise, California 95969, USA). Both claim extensive coverage and are full of interesting comment and data on the multitude of periodicals they cover. The Dustbooks volume grew out of the *International Directory of Little Magazines and Small Presses*, now in its twentieth year, which lists tens of thousands of English-language periodicals worldwide including at least 1170 small mags claiming to be devoted only to poetry. The problem with all three directories is that they are American — strong on home-grown markets, weak and distant in their coverage of ours.

● *Small Presses And Little Magazines of the UK and Ireland — An Address List*. A regularly updated listing of more than 1000 addresses put out by Oriel Bookshop with the assistance of the ALP. Copies cost £5.50 by post from Oriel, The Friary, Cardiff, CF1 4AA.

● *British Literary Periodicals — A Selected Bibliography*. The British Council's guide to the less ephemeral magazines, many of which publish poetry. Copies from 10 Spring Gardens, London SW1A 2BN.

● *The little magazines themselves*. Most give details of other periodicals in their "publications received" page, some quite extensively. Particularly good are *Orbis* (199 The Long Shoot, Nuneaton, Warwickshire) who run a quarterly poetry index ,compiled by Edna Eglinton, and *The Poetry Review* (21 Earls Court Square, London SW5) which for the past few years have been printing round-ups of regional poetry activity. Magazines are a good way of keeping up to date. Track one to the next, they spread out across the world like radio hams.

● *The Poetry Library*, Currently the finest and most accessible collection of contemporary poetry in the country. Recent magazines can be consulted, obscure ones can be traced. Handlist available. See Appendix 3.

● *The Poetry Society*, 21 Earl's Court Square, London SW5. In addition to bringing out its own magazine, *The Poetry Review*, the Society offers publishing advice and produces a list of recent magazines.

● *Specialist bookshops* (listed in Appendix 1). Most of these can supply poetry mags by post or can be visited for a thorough browsing. Try asking the managers which magazines they'd recommend.

- *Greeting Card and Calendar Association* (6 Wimpole Street, London W1M 8AS) produces a list of members, some of which accept light verse.

- *Writing For The BBC* (BBC Publications — available through bookshops, £3.99): "A guide to writers on possible markets for their work."

- *Regional Arts Associations* (see Appendix 3). Many publish a local arts or literary magazine — *People To People*, *The Printer's Devil*, etc — and all can give details of poetry magazines operating in their regions.

Once you begin to delve into addresses, the possible markets will seem immense. Move quickly — keep your ear to the ground. Find out which magazines appear to publish indifferent work from the famous while ignoring good material from the newly begun. Learn to spot the innovative and adventurous periodicals, those which hunt out new talent and are prepared especially to take the risks of publishing the unknown.

7
Rejection

Rejection slips are like colds; everybody gets them, some people *catch* them more often than others.
Norman Hidden

The most usual result of sending your poems in is to have them sent back again. Rejection. It comes like a slap in the face, you don't expect it, don't deserve it. Why you? The common reaction is to blame the editor, the magazine, the system, anything bar the poems. Around you are hundreds of other writers — all being rejected in the same offhand way. There is a sense of common injustice in all this. It should sustain you as you grumble through the morning, completely put off. It seems doubly unfair that rejections should come so early — often the first thing you hear on waking is the *thwap* of your poems coming home to roost. Rejections are painful. It is *you* who have been turned down, *you* who have been daubed as not good enough.

But let's put this in perspective. Does rejection mean that the work is inferior? Are the poems really not up to scratch? In many cases, unfortunately so. Many poets submit work that they know is unfinished, that is weak, unexciting, that they recognize as flawed, sometimes that they do not themselves even like. They imagine, I suppose, that someone else will find their second-rate creations worthwhile. It doesn't happen, of course. Only famous poets can get by on bad poems and even there the fame eventually wears out.

It is worth looking at exactly what standard is aimed for. The only specific, often quoted by editors when defining their needs, is the phrase "good poetry" — and what is that? There is no unassailable standard of goodness; the term changes according to fashion and to the recommendations and predilections of those poets who sell more than others at any specific time. Good poetry — you cannot even look back through literary history to find it. That too changes in importance, according to the whims of the age which does the judging. So what does it mean, this subjective average? What the editor likes, I suppose, what he or she decides to use.

All writers of good work have at some stage had it rejected. There is no universal scale of quality against which they can be measured.

If we take novelists as an example we find J.P. Donleavy's classic *The Ginger Man* rejected 36 times, James Joyce's *Dubliners* turned down 22 times and John Creasey, who wrote 564 books under 13 pen names, receiving 743 rejection slips before his mystery novels took off. So what does it really matter that *your* poems have come back?

> The number of rejections could have no bearing on the validity of the poem . . .
>
> C.H. Sisson

There are many reasons why rejection takes place and the sheer volume of poetry received by poetry magazines is undoubtedly high on the list. *Outposts* receives 83,000 poems a year, *Poetry Review* gets 20,000 and even much smaller magazines can manage to see four or five thousand. Out of this huge input of verse as few as 120 are printed by *Outposts*, 130 with *Poetry Review* and perhaps only 60 with a smaller journal such as *Momentum*. This is less than half a percent.

Mike Shields of *Orbis* reckons that in addition to being almost overwhelmed by the volume of submissions three-quarters of what arrives is sent back because it is wrong. It is too long, too late for a special issue, unsuitable — the magazine uses no experimental poetry for example but still finds it submitted, or contains obviously flawed technique — missed rhymes, uneven meters. Of the quantity remaining four-fifths gets returned because of lack of space:

> All good, competent and often likeable in itself. Rejected poems, then, haven't fallen short of some eternal standard; they just didn't match a temporary need. Even failure is relative.

Some editors send everything back once they've got enough in hand for a specific issue. Others clear the decks periodically — even sending back good work — in order to give themselves space to breathe. Generally, though, the main reason is incorrect submission. You haven't studied the magazine, you've sent in the wrong kind of stuff.

In a survey I carried out among a good cross-section of British poets I discovered that everyone had suffered rejection at some time and no one had regarded a poem's return as a reason for giving it up. Most agreed that a rejected poem should be tried again elsewhere, repeatedly, until it bored or new work had taken its place. Peter Redgrove remarked that publication in a contemporary magazine was not necessarily a corroboration of the poem's success. Like C.H. Sisson he believes the validation to be elsewhere.

How should you react then? Collect the rejection slips — mostly small squares of paper bearing a printed regret from the editor, plus the magazine's name and address — pin them on your notice board, or, as certain poets possessed of a kind of submission mania have done, paper your wall with them. Generally speaking these slips will bear no comment but if they do, feel encouraged. Some editors are more willing to spend their time this way than others. If yours has a remark on it, *read it*. Don't tear it off and throw it in the fire. It is unlikely that you will alter your poem as a result of criticisms but it may put you in a more commanding position when you write the next.

If your poems come back in batches one after another try not to get paranoid. Don't worry about what the postman may think. He doesn't care. Think of it like juggling; as poems return, pack them up again and send them out elsewhere. Do remember to remove the rejection slip — it's been known for poets to forget. If the MS becomes tatty or overfolded, retype it. Keep it looking new. Try not to become obsessive about publication. Do not endlessly bombard the same magazine with packet after packet of verse. Jeremy Silver of *Strange Mathematics* says of such poets: "They seem to think editors are some kind of enemy to be engaged in a war of attrition — these writers unfortunately also tend to be the least discriminating and self-critical in their own work." Spread your shots — the target is large enough. Surviving rejection is a test of your seriousness.

> If a poet realizes that it has been his privilege to have a certain gift in the manipulation of language (language being the supreme human manifestation) then he is obviously committed from the very beginning to a life time of self-discipline, struggle, disappointment, failure, with just possibly that odd success which is greater in his eyes than it probably is in the eyes of anyone else.
>
> R.S. Thomas, *Selected Prose*

And if your ultimate goal is your own book then that "odd success", a well-written poem published in a small magazine, is a vital step on the way.

Reputations are fragile things. They don't come easily and they don't come overnight. Build yours by perseverance and determination and, most importantly, by creating competent work. Rejections never stop but they can be encouraged to slow down.

8

The Book-Length Manuscript

You are ready for your first slim volume. Poetry collections are habitually slim, sometimes too thin to have the title printed on their spines. If you imagined a fat book — hundreds of pages — it won't turn out like that. It can take good poets a lifetime to bulk their works enough to make them stand collected without bookends. Not all poets do this — over the years Robert Graves consistently reduced his. He became dissatisfied with the earlier verses and took the opportunity to remove them at each reprint. Most poets, though, will want to chuck everything in. TAKE CARE. Once your book is printed it will be around a long time to haunt you. In fifteen or twenty years' time, with a settled reputation, you hope, early faltering can creep back into the public eye via a diligent critic writing up your career. At a lesser level, friends may discover what you used to be like and embarrass you with it when you were trying to forget. Many poets get caught like this. They omit the names of their early pamphlets from their biographical notes. They regret what they've done, pretend it was someone else. Check with a reference library to spot them — a graveyard of disowned books.

American critic John Haines comments:

> Too many of the poems written by young people these days suffer from unripeness, from the hastiness that rushing into print encourages. What we want in a poem is not some half-baked comment that any momentarily inspired ass might make, but a piece of work — let's call it *art* which embodies in a memorable way, through its sound, the images it presents, its rhythmical solidity and intensity, a part of our lives, recognizable and hidden; and which at the same time offers us in its contained beauty, its grace of structure and expression, an alternative to the ugliness and stupidity, the emptiness and triviality of which our life is too often made. Frankly this is not what I get from reading [contemporary poetry].

And at root what he's talking about is books. Magazines are transient, they fade away. Books have a dogged determination to stay on people's shelves.

One answer is to do what Emily Dickinson did and keep your poems in a trunk, or follow Gillian Clarke's example and do nothing at all with them for years until you are sure you are ready. But when is ready? Don't attempt to bring out a book until you've been writing poetry for five years. Plenty of practice, that's one solution. I would imagine, though, that most poets will be more impatient than that.

As you assemble the book, ask yourself a few questions. Why? What keeps these poems together? Is there a theme? Are you merely showing people what you can do? Are there too many? Is it too long? Can you cut it down? Take it slowly. If in doubt, leave it out. If the poem needs rewriting then do it. Don't accept the half-successful. Take advice — rope in others to check your selection, ask them if it works as a book and if they say it's uneven or express any shade of doubt go back and consider the whole thing again yourself.

This is a collection of poems, not an anthology. Local journalists wilfully misuse the word "anthology". It's from the Greek, originally referring to a collection of epigrams; it now means a selection of poems of a common type or on a common theme made by one person from the work of others. The word "book" can cause trouble too. I've heard quite substantial volumes referred to as booklets, stiff-covered chapbooks dismissed as leaflets and what is clearly a four-page pamphlet proudly referred to as a book. It all depends, I suppose, on where you happen to be on the escalator of achievement. For the purposes of Public Lending Right a book of poetry must be both printed and bound as well as offered for sale. UNESCO demands a minimum number of pages. It makes sense, otherwise we'd end up with greetings cards on the shelves of public libraries, bits of paper given Standard Book Numbers and matchbox labels up for the Booker Prize. The average slim volume of verse by a new poet is around 50 pages and contains between 25 and 30 poems. Unless you have exceptional reasons, try to make your selection conform to that.

Presentation

Presentation for submission to a publisher is not complicated. Avoid being fussy. Prepare each poem as if for magazine submission, omitting your name and address from each sheet. Give some thought to order, particularly the final poem. This should give a kind of completeness to the selection, a rounding-off rather than a stopping in mid-air. Groups of short poems dispersed among longer pieces will assist the flow. Divide the selection thematically if you can. If that won't work, run the poems sequentially, in order of date of composition. If you've employed similar images in different poems put them at opposite ends of the collection or leave one out altogether. Don't be afraid to rearrange the contents a number of times until you get it right. A lot of readers won't follow your order anyway — they'll dip and skip. Ignore them. Prepare your selection in the best shape you can.

The book should begin with a title-page which includes your name and most importantly your address. You can follow with a dedication — not too lengthy for risk of sounding pretentious — and a list of acknowledgements as to previous publication if you have any. Something along the lines of:

> Some of the poems in this collection have previously appeared in *Poetry Ireland Review, Mar, Stand, Poetry Review, Poetry (USA)*, and have been broadcast on Radio 4. "Dog days" was a winner in the Cardiff International Poetry Competition.

This will suffice. Don't go into lengthy detail of exactly what and exactly when, thanking each editor by name. This, too, can sound ostentatious. The purpose of acknowledgements is to impress both the publisher and the reader and to convince them that the poetry is valid. They are credentials if you like. Do not include acknowledgements for publication which has not yet occurred: a lot can go wrong between acceptance letter and the magazine actually coming out. Include a contents sheet, listing each poem by title, in the order in which they are to appear. Don't forget the poems themselves, of course; and finally add a few biographical notes about yourself which could be used on the flyleaf or back jacket.

Make this simple. It's very easy to go over the top when you are describing yourself. Remarks like "Eschews tradition and intends fervently to change the future with his poetry" will sound pretty silly in ten years' time when it's obvious that you haven't. Date and place of birth, education, what you do, any special *literary* achievements rather than less relevant personal ones, perhaps a quote from a literary figure about your poetry, if you've been lucky enough to get one, or maybe a remark or two about how and what you write. Most likely nothing of this kind will readily spring to mind, in which case don't labour it. Nothing is obligatory. I once knew a poet who admitted that he found the biographical note harder to write than the poems; in the end he did without. Here is a simple biographical note taken from Lotte Moos's *Time to be Bold*, published by Centerprise:

> Lotte Moos is a founder member of the Hackney Writers Workshop. She's been writing fables, poems, stories since she was a child. Has worked

as a photographer, nursemaid, typist, got herself through evening school, span (wool), taught, translated, interpreted and brought up two children.

Since joining the Hackney Writers Workshop in 1976 has written a great many funny and not so funny poems, some of which are contained in the present volume.

When you've got all your pages together, read them again to make sure the poems still work, that you've removed all the bumps, that you are completely satisfied with what you intend to let loose on the world. Put in another sheet at the end for luck containing your name and address again in case the publisher mislays it, number each page consecutively and clip them in the top left-hand corner with a wire staple or filing pin. Do not go in for hardbacked folders or special bindings. As Sir Stanley Unwin said: "A complete MS tastefully bound in morocco would fill me with as much distrust as would an overdressed dandy. I should feel confident that that was the only form in which the manuscript was destined to be preserved."

You might have the idea that your book of poems should be illustrated. You know an artist, (or you are an artist yourself) who could do the job very well. Publishers do not take kindly to MSS turning up accompanied by oil paintings or slides which they won't have a viewer for, or photographs which would make the book very expensive to print. There are exceptions: Ted Hughes's *River* accompanied by Peter Keen's photographs and his *Remains of Elmet — A Pennine Sequence* with those of Fay Goodwin are marvellous composite achievements. R.S. Thomas's sequence of poems *Between Here and Now*, inspired by Impressionist paintings in the Louvre, would have lost a lot if reproductions of the works had not faced the verses. Both Michael Horovitz's *Growing Up: Selected Poems 1951-79* and Stevie Smith's *Collected Poems* are interlaced with the poet's doodles, "idiosyncratic drawings, used where appropriate" — and they do illuminate the work. But generally this is a luxury. Leave it until you are better known.

If you are thinking of using a *nom de plume*, a pseudonym, don't. It is an affectation. Unless you are entering a competition where it is a requisite or you happen to be famous in another sphere of public life and wish to versify anonymously, use the name you've been given. If that itself is awful you'll have changed it by deed poll by now anyway. Some romantic novelists write so many books that for reasons of public credibility they have been forced to adopt aliases, in some cases half a dozen or more. As far as I am aware this does not happen with poetry. Stick to your real name — it will help sell your book to the neighbours.

Title

And the title. What have you called your selection? Sometimes this is obvious, it will leap at you. More often though it is a problem. Booksellers will tell you that titles are important, they help the impulse purchase, and anything that encourages people to actually pick up a book is worth serious consideration. It may be that a single poem in the collection has a gripping title. If so, use that. Perhaps there is a thematic connection you can embroider. Do not take the obvious and easy way out. Your title has a job to do.

Here is a list of rotten titles that don't do anything to make you want to look inside the books and sound like the quick afterthoughts which they obviously are: *Singing Verses*, *Mostly Modern*, *Poetic Gems*, *Nineteen Fragments*, *Season's Verses*, *Poetic Memories*, *Selected Rhymes*, *Poetic Gleanings*, *Collected Thoughts*, *Random Reflections*, *Summer Idylls*, *Mood Meditation*, *Poems in Many Voices*, *Poetic Thoughts*, *Varied Poetic Thoughts*, *Ten Poems*, *Eighteen Poems*, *Twenty-Five Poems*. The poet who used the last two was Dylan Thomas but that doesn't excuse him. Fey labels like these will not help your book. Avoid them. Readers are not generally interested in *Varied Poetic Thoughts*, even if that is all you have to offer. Call them something else.

A little better is to use a vague, amorphous generalization: *Affinities*, *Voices*, *Soundings*, *Trails*, *Songs*, *Celebrations*, *Dialogues*, *Landmarks*, *Turns*, *Crossings*, *Moments of Grace*, *Variations*, *Arrangements*, *Roots and Branches*, *Forays*, *Threads*, *Workings* — all taken from books by respected poets yet they still don't sound really like anything worth reading.

Some poets invent names or use little-encountered words: *Bill Jubobe*, *Pleats*, *Ziggurats*, *Kaddish*, *Slembic*, *Ere-Voice*, *Witt*, *Zadar*, *Tetraktys*, *Antarktika*, *Rasgos*, *Citrinas*, *Kurrirrurrirri*, *Imbrications*, *Logotrickades*, *Grotesca*, *Imstanit Mhash*. The idea of startling the potential reader with something unusual is fine but there are so many like this at the modernist end of the poetry shelves that really nothing stands out.

The best titles are individual, unorthodox, apposite for their content yet unexpected labeling for a book of poems. Here are some of my favourites:

> *Play the Piano Drunk Like a Percussion Instrument Until the Fingers Begin to Bleed a Bit* — Charles Bukowski.
> *The Deceptive Grin of the Gravel Porters* — Gavin Ewart.

The Green Desert — Harri Webb (poems about depopulated mid-Wales).

The Lonely Suppers of W.V. Balloon — Christopher Middleton (surrealist verse).

Dr Faust's Sea-Spiral Spirit — Peter Redgrove.

Seven Elephants and One Eye — Tim Longville.

The Shameless Hussy — Alta (feminist verse).

English Subtitles — Peter Porter (reminding us that he is Australian).

Old Maps and New — Norman MacCaig (so much slicker than "New and Selected Verse").

H'm — R.S. Thomas (an onomatopoeic title aptly condensing the poet's attitude to us all).

When Meic Stephens and I had finished editing a new anthology of poetry by the younger writers of Wales we sat around for days chucking names at each other — *Yellow Rocks*, *New Fruits*, *Fresh Rushes*, *Green Souls* — we went through the contents list, the index of first lines, the telephone book, directories of small magazines. Nothing. In the end we called it *Green Horse* from a line Meic Stephens found in Pablo Neruda's *Memoirs*. It had little to do with Wales but the celtic overtones of "greenness" and "horses" seemed to work. When you can't think of a title yourself, don't give up. Have a look through what others have done.

Submitting your manuscript

If you think your collection is ready, pack it up like a magazine submission, adding extra postage to cover the weight. Make a copy for yourself — title-pages, everything — in case it gets lost. Where do you send it?

Most poets at their first attempt try the commercial publishing houses (see Chapter 9). And as commercial publishers will tell you, most of the MSS they receive get sent back. Hardly ever do they "discover" someone new, like that, out of the blue. Yet this doesn't stop hundreds of poets up and down the country submitting their collected, previously unpublished works in the hope that they've got it, that they'll make it, that the intellectual hero dust will come down on them and make them sages, geniuses, artists or whatever else they expected from poetic triumph overnight. There *are* slim chances but it would be a lot easier on both poet and publisher if there were not.

Unless you have a reputation and there is some expectation that your books will sell, don't bother trying the big boys. You might be outstanding — and we all think at times that our poems are outstanding — but you'll need more than the agreement of your aunt to convince a publisher.

If you are determined and are certain that you are ready, that your work is accomplished and that there is a market for it, then go ahead. The best introduction to outstanding work is the work itself. Send it in without fuss or embellishment, with the simplest of covering letters, and wait. The publisher will read it, or the publisher's editor will. If they don't feel qualified to judge, or if they are rushed, or if it's a borderline case for acceptance then it might be sent to an outside reader — a critic or fellow poet — for a report. Don't expect to read this; it's like a building society surveyor's report — a document of vital importance to yourself which you're never allowed to see.

Expect to wait two weeks or two months — sometimes longer — before you get a reply. In some cases, though, you just don't hear — for month after month. Since not all publishers acknowledge receipt of MSS it might be worth enquiring after three months of silence if your book actually arrived. But leave it at that. Don't pester. Silence can be ominous or no news can be good news. You'll just have to wait. Most likely when you do hear it'll be a simple printed rejection. Don't worry, don't write back, don't complain. It's happened to hundreds of writers — Theodore Dreiser, James Joyce, Herman Melville, Daniel Defoe, Arnold Bennett, Edward Fitzgerald with his translation of *The Rubaiyát of Omar Khayyám*, Zane Grey — they've all sent books in just to have them summarily thrown back.

You may think the publisher hasn't read it. "If he'd read he would have accepted. I don't understand." Some poets become obsessive about this — laying traps for the publisher by inserting hairs, bits of tape, pages in upside down or whatever — just to be able to say, "Well, I told you so." They forget the truth of Dr Johnson's remark that "it is unnecessary to eat the whole ox to find out whether the beef is tough". It does happen, publishers do not necessarily read all your poems — a few may be enough to tell them that your book won't suit. Don't complain. They are not obligated to you: you chose to approach them, they didn't ask you to send your work in. They may be wrong, exhibit poor judgement, appear insulting, all of these things. Leave them. Replace the title-page on your book to maintain crispness and send it off

46

to someone else. Keep records. To whom sent, when, how long it took coming back.

Your determination will be driven by your expectation. If you believe you are worth it and that it can be done then keep trying. No one ever won by giving up.

9
Markets — The Book

Commercially it is a small one. Despite what you may read in the Sunday papers and allowing for a few notable exceptions — Phillip Larkin, Fiona Pitt-Kethley, Irina Ratushinskaya, Roger McGough, Ted Hughes, Seamus Heaney — poetry does not sell in large quantities. Compared to books on gardening, cookery or romantic novels it is a non-starter. Its continuing attraction for a small number of British publishers remains a mystery. Perhaps they, like the poets, do it because they have to, although it is more likely that they do it to add weight to their lists, to put back into the system a little of what capitalist hype and bestseller manipulation has taken out. In 1989 from a total of 3,652 publishers there were 898 books of poetry published; of this quantity 104 were reprints and 83 translations. This is effectively 711 new poetry titles — a fair number you may think, but not when taken in the context of the UK output as a whole. That was 61,195.

Who are they then, these barons who take risks for a bit of high art, to help them get their hard heads through the night? Actually there are not very many — three commercial houses who could be said to actively encourage poetry, twelve or more who do it sometimes, four or five subsidized specialists and of course the small presses. Don't underestimate these; in volumes terms they publish the most.

The main output comes traditionally from *Faber and Faber* (an influence of T.S. Eliot's) and here only one new, untried poet — if that — is taken on a year. The other principal publishing houses are *Secker and Warburg*, *Hutchinson*, *Chatto and Windus* and the *Oxford University Press*, all with active lists, all taking on first time poets — but never those without a reputation. Other important companies include *Allison and Busby*, *Jonathan Cape*, *Collins Harvill*, *Hamish Hamilton*, *Unwin Hyman*, *Blackstaff Press*, *Mainstream Publishing*, *Gomer Press*, all with poetry in their catologues, although new names do not get added that often.

Other publishing houses do publish poetry: *Macmillan*, *Dent*, *Andre Deutsch*, etc — although their lists have been so reduced in recent years that their interest could now be said to be in retreat. The recent trend has been for a revival of interest by mass-market paperback houses — notably *Penguin* and *Paladin* — in putting well produced and competitively priced volumes before the general public. As well as having a long standing interest in anthologies — *The Penguin Book Of Victorian Verse*, *The Penguin Book of Zen Poetry*, *The Penguin Book of Contemporary British Poetry*, etc — Penguin have also expanded their list of classic poets — Wordsworth, Betjeman, Whitman — to include a series of comprehensive selections from the outputs of contemporary writers like Peter Redgrove, U.A. Fanthorpe, Roger McGough, Andrew Motion, James Fenton and Jeremy Reed. In addition they produce an extensive range of anthologies and collections for children. This is no arena for beginners, however, almost everyone published has established themselves previously elsewhere. *Paladin* — part of the Collins-Grafton-Fontana group — have adopted a different approach. Following in the wake of their controversial and most distinctly non-mainstream anthology *The New British Poetry* they have published a stream of poets whose reputations rest not with the centre but rather the fringe: Iain Sinclair, Tom Raworth, Lee Harwood, and others now sit on bookshop shelves next to volumes by Philip Larkin and W.B. Yeats.

Both the *Women's Press* and *Virago*, keen to be seen as publishers of work from all genres, have also dabbled with poetry as have the *Gay Men's Press* but as of yet no concerted policy has emerged.

The real growth during the past decade has been among the specialists — *Bloodaxe*, *Carcanet*, *Seren Books* (formerly *Poetry Wales Press*), *Littlewood*, *Enitharmon*, *The Gallery Press*, *Peterloo Poets*, *Anvil Press* — indeed *Bloodaxe* probably publish more new poetry per year than all the commercial companies put together. Begun often by one person these enterprises have developed with the help of public subsidy and managerial flair to fill the middle ground between part-time pamphleteering and full-scale commercial publishing at a national level. Some of them — notably *Carcanet* — already operate with commerce in mind if not exactly in response to market forces. A number use professional warehousing, representation and have national distribution. Their books are first class, rivalling the best productions of their more commercial counterparts. Their motivation is what drives them, often with missionary zeal, putting poetry before profit. They are accordingly much more open to the newcomer, to the less-tried poet with a good collection to hand.

The small presses — 600 or more in the UK — spread out across the base of the pyramid. It is here where the real risks — creative rather than commercial — are run. Little presses range, like little magazines, through the full spectrum of production quality and content. Many are spin-offs from magazines following a particular predeliction in more specialist form. Others exist to further the editor's interests or the work of a founding group. They are basically open but if you mail poetry to them do not expect regular commercial practice to hold sway. MSS get considered but it's haphazard. Write first to check out the ground.

A little press is "little" because of its form of organization — usually one person running the whole operation as a hobby or obsession part-time. Jeff Nuttall in *PALPI* argues against the nomenclature:

> In the old days, when there was but one way of writing poetry and the little presses published slighter or preparatory work by exactly the same people as were published in the big presses, then "little" was a fitting word maybe. Nowadays the quiet revolution that has happened in the little presses means that they carry the burden of a massive literary flowering, whilst the established (big) publishing houses carry next to nothing of value. "Little" is therefore a misnomer.

In the end it is a matter of degree although by their default the commercial publishers have tended to add weight to Nuttall's critique. The value attributed to poetry, as I've pointed out before, depends considerably on where the critic stands.

Small presses currently, or at least recently, publishing individual collections of poetry include *Allardyce, Barnett, Raven Arts, Agenda Editions, Diamond, Fleeting Monolith, 4-Eyes, Mannamead, Writers Forum, Pig, Poet and Printer, Red Shark, Oleander, Galloping Dog Press, Hippopotamus, Taxus, Stride, BB Books, Amra Imprint, B4, Chiron, Dangaroo, Excess, Mir Poets, Wellsweep, Toad's Damp Press, Morning Star, Mammon, Lark Lane Poetry Books, Honno, Hub Editions, Iron, Headland, Hard Pressed Poetry, Hangman Books, North and South, Prebendal, Smith/Doorstop, Zanzibar Productions, Dedalus* and *Childe Roland*. There is no priority in this sequence. It stops at risk of boring you; as with the little magazines on page 33 the list could go on and on.

The small presses are the home of the "bold experimental and explorative writing that is essential to any vitality in modern literature" (*Print Out* leaflet, Eastern Arts Association). There are also so many of them that the aspiring poet is bound to stand a better chance. Read widely. Make sure you know what's going on.

It would be little use for me here to recommend the best publishers to receive the MSS of your first volume. Fashions change, considerations shift. Small presses alter from day to day. In any event one or two recommended publishers would receive so many MSS that they would be swamped. Spread the market, stretch out as far as you can. Don't necessarily try the obvious. New publishers who have never touched poetry before may be interested — be persistent, try them. The worst that can happen is for your book to get sent back.

But remember, *don't submit blindly*. Always find out first what a particular publisher's books are actually like.

Sources for addresses

● *The Writers' and Artists' Yearbook* (A. & C. Black).

● *Cassell and the Publishers Association Directory of Publishing* (Cassell).

● *The Writer's Handbook* (Macmillan)

● *The Small Press Yearbook* (Small Press Group of Britain, BM Bozo, London WC1N 3XX).

● *Small Presses and Little Magazines of the UK — An Address List* (Oriel)

● *Catalogue of Small Press Books in Print* (Association of Little Presses, 89a Petherton Road, London N5 2QT).

● The familiar listings in *PALPI* and the backs of little magazines.

10
Copyright

Copyright is one of the literary world's most misspelt words. It deals with the *right* of copying, not the *wright* of making nor the *write* of recording the information, of getting it down. It is also one of the most misunderstood. There are a welter of acts, conventions, precedents and provisions to confuse you and they get more complex as you probe. Successful novelists leave it to their agents: "It's how they earn their 10 per cent." But most poets will need a basic grasp of the subject, since if there's any defending to do they'll have to manage on their own.

Plagiarism

First let's dispose of an urban myth — the ever-present imitator who steals your ideas as soon as you scribble them down. I'm always coming up against this one, the sob-story of an unprotected work filched from under the poet's nose. Usually the poem has been sent in somewhere — to a magazine or maybe a radio programme — and nothing has been heard. Later the same piece, changed slightly, resurfaces with another's name on it and the real poet gets no acknowledgement at all. In my experience this just doesn't happen. When I investigate these stories — and I've done this more than once — the facts melt, the magazines dissolve. "Ah, so it wasn't the *South East Review* he sent it to then, must have been elsewhere." And that's another thing, I notice that it is never the person telling the story that it's happened to either — it's always someone else.

Actually plagiarism is a matter of degree. Ben Johnson remarks that one of the requisites of the poet is to imitate, "to be able to convert the substance or riches of another poet to his own use". But it does depend on how far you go. In the 1960s the Scottish poet Hugh MacDiarmid published a poem entitled "Perfect" about a gull's wing. Its text was almost word for word taken from a short story by Anglo-Welsh author Glyn Jones. In the ensuing correspondence published by *The Times Literary Supplement* MacDiarmid claimed to have a photographic memory and to have used the Glyn Jones story unconsciously. He failed to retract the work none the less and you can find it today in his collected poems.

Generally speaking, however, poetry is free of such copyright infringers. There are borrowers, certainly, but the wholesale misappropriation of another's work and the passing off of that as your own is rare. In the twentieth century the concept of total and exclusive originality has loomed in importance. Previous eras accepted it as normal that themes, ideas, images would be rewritten and reused by succeeding generations of writers. Today there is something about mass literacy and mass communication which makes it apparently essential for any creative work to be yours and yours alone.

How copyright is established

The biggest myth about copyright in Britain is that you have to do something to obtain it, to register it as your own. This misunderstanding comes in part from America, where at one time copyright could only be obtained via registration, and from our own Copyright Act of 1911 which requires publishers to deliver copies of all new books to certain deposit libraries, free of charge. It is the practice of some to send a copy of their poetry by registered mail to a bank where it is kept, unopened, in the strong-room. This establishes the work as theirs beyond a doubt, as well as recording the date of composition. This is worth doing if you can afford it or feel especially at risk but it's not *necessary* at all.

Copyright obtains at the moment a poem is created. Write out the words and the copyright is yours. Half-finish the poem and that part is copyright. Your notes are copyright, your scratched image on the back of a beermat is copyright. And you need do nothing to claim that right at all. In Britain copyright law is contained in the 1989 Copyright, Design and Patents Act which restates and replaces the earlier 1956 Copyright Act adding, among other things, the new "moral" right to be identified as the author of a work. The law provides for the protection of a writer's poetry but not the ideas or the images or the sense of that poetry. Copyright covers the actual form and style of the words, rather than what they say. This protection is yours until you die, when it passes to your estate and then persists for a further fifty years before emerging into the public domain. This means that your work cannot be used without your permission for a considerable time. If there is still an interest in it half a century after you've gone then the nation deserves it for nothing. You'll be part of the culture by then.

What can you do with your copyright? If you think of it as property, which is how the law regards it, then you can sell it, lease it, lend it or even give it away. If you submit a poem to a magazine and the work is used the copyright usually stays with you. Even if you've been paid, the copyright remains yours. Only if you actually sign your copyright away can it pass to another. Generally speaking this doesn't happen with magazines and the rule would be not to sign anything — unless of course you're being offered plenty of cash.

Magazines and anthologies often display a copyright symbol © thus:

© 1983 Bonzo Dog Publications

Don't be alarmed. This symbol isn't necessary, as I've pointed out, to gain protection under British law but it will help gain protection abroad, particularly in America, where copyright conventions are different. Secondly it is only the *selection* of the anthology or magazine — the choice of works and the order in which they run — which is being claimed. Copyright remains with the copyright holders — be they the poets or some other individual, usually a publisher, to whom the rights have been sold. A full copyright notice, found on the verso (that's the back) of the title-page, ought to look like this:

I HAVE NO GUN BUT I CAN SPIT
Edited by Kenneth Baker
Copyright © 1980 by Kenneth Baker
Individual poems © as indicated in Acknowledgements.

The acknowledgements will then go on to show, for example, that Kingsley Amis owns the poems taken "from *Collected Poems 1944–1979* © 1978 by Kingsley Amis", and Christopher Logue owns the two poems "© 1969 and 1980 by Christopher Logue", and so on. So there is a double protection: to you for your poem and then to the editor for his or her selection.

The situation could be different with a collection of poems sold to a publisher. It may well be a term of your contract that copyright should pass to the publisher, in which case your rights would leave you forever. If this is to be the case, then weigh judgement with care. You would be offered a fee rather than a royalty and that would be that. No matter how successful your work, nor how many copies printed, you would receive nothing further. In fact the new copyright holder — the publisher — could alter your work as he or she saw fit and you would have no recourse. But this is far-fetched, it rarely happens.

Quotation

What are important are the *rights* to your published work and the *permissions* required to quote from it or to use it again. The really difficult problems occur with fiction, of course, involving film and television rights, but poetry can be complex enough. Once published it may well be that your work will be selected for anthology appearance, for use on the stage in some verse presentation, be broadcast, or even used as part of a critical treatise or text book. In most cases permission will be required from the copyright holder for the poem's use and this invariably means the payment of a fee. They'll write to you (depending on the terms of your publishing agreement, the granting of permissions for anthology use and the resulting fees may have to be shared with your publisher). However, the Copyright Acts do allow certain circumstances where permission for use of copyright material need *not* be sought. These are roughly as follows:

(a)   For use in research and private study.
(b)   For use in criticism and review.
(c)   For the recording of current events.
(d)   Reproduction for a judicial proceeding.
(e)   Reading aloud in public, (but not broadcast, or recorded).
(f)   Inclusion, under certain circumstances, of a short extract in a collection intended for schools.

A "less than substantial" part of a work may also be used in other circumstances without permission.

The Society of Authors and the Publishers Association have laid down guidelines as to the lengths of quotation below which permission is not needed. These are as follows: an extract of less than 40 lines or a series of extracts totalling the same, an extract of less than a quarter of the complete poem or series of extracts totalling the same. Quotation of this length can be made without informing you so long as an acknowledgement of the copyright holder is included. This, however, is only a convention and has no actual legal standing. It has been established on the one hand to allow fair use of published material and on the other to protect the copyright holder who might find himself or herself quoted at inordinate length with no acknowledgement or payment at all.

Infringement

What can you do if you feel that the law has been broken? What remedies are there for infringement? What should you do? First make sure of your facts. Copyright law, as I've pointed out, can be a minefield for the uninitiated. Read up on it — the Acts and conventions themselves if you can manage it, *Copinger and Skone James on Copyright* (Sweet & Maxwell) or Laddie, Prescott and Vitoria *The Modern Law of Copyright* (Butterworths) and at very least Amanda L. Michael's succinct contribution "British Copyright Law" in the *Writer's And Artist's Yearbook* (A & C Black). If you think you have a case consult your solicitor and if the solicitor advises it, sue. Personally, unless it involved a great deal of cash, I wouldn't waste my time. I'd use it to write a few new poems instead.

11
Cash

Payment to the poet for publication hardly exists. Most little magazines pay nothing at all, excepting free contributor's copies, and even then they encourage poets to subscribe. Small presses bringing out your first collection expect you to be satisfied with the kudos — you'll receive half a dozen free author's copies maybe and then be obliged to help promote the sales of the rest. A few poetry magazines, inevitably those with sponsorship of some sort, pay a small amount per page. This is usually around £2 although some of those attracting heavier grants manage a bit more.

Publication of a poem in one of the non-specialist periodicals, the review monthlies or the newspapers, can earn more. Rates vary — between £20 and £50 a poem is normal, with a bit more from prestige markets such as the quality Sundays.

Rates for inclusion in anthologies are unusual in that they have a basic *minimum* agreed between the Society of Authors and the Publishers Association. This is a UK and Commonwealth rate of £30 for the first ten lines; £1.50 per line for the next twenty and £1.00 a line subsequently. The rate may reduce by one-third if the poem appears in a literary or scholarly journal or an anthology that contains more than forty poems in copyright, or has a print run of less than 1500 copies. These rates are minimums, established poets will negotiate more. American and World rights command at least half as much again. In practice these rates are exceeded by some of the better publishers and totally ignored by the rest.

Collections of poetry from established publishers warrant an agreement involving a royalty payment — usually 10 per cent of the cover price on every copy sold (though 7½ per cent is common for a paperback edition) — and the poet gets an advance roughly equivalent to the expected sales in the first year. This can be £300 if your prospects are good.

Quite exceptionally the BBC, due in part to its agreement with the Publishers Association, pays reasonably well. Network radio will bring £8.55 per half minute and television £15.50. In addition if the poet reads the work himself a performance fee is paid. Local radio broadcasts gain 25 per cent of the network rate. These are minimum rates. Poets of high standing are often able to negotiate more.

Generally speaking, though, you can see that if it's money you want you'd be better off writing jokes for the backs of matchboxes. An issue of *The Author* quotes a distinguished poet on the economic problems of his art:

I calculate, roughly, that in an average year my principal sources of income are, in *approximate* percentage terms:

1.	Published poems in magazines	5
2.	Earnings from published books	5
3.	Poetry readings and talks etc.	40
4.	Broadcast poems	5
5.	Other work for radio (e.g. schools)	20
6.	Journalism: reviewing, radio, etc.	15
7.	Other	10

— in other words, poets *can't* earn enough just from writing, publishing and broadcasting poems. You have to work very hard at the readings and performances, at connected BBC work, at reviewing. What often alarms me is that if readings dried up . . . and if a few magazines closed, and if Radio 3 was shut down, three-quarters of my income would vanish.

Moreover, I can keep up at 50 a punishing schedule of readings and lectures for comparatively low fees (I ask on average £40)* — 54 readings in 1981. But how long will I have the appetite and energy for this?

* The rate for a public reading in 1991 for better known poets would be £70 or more.

Newer and less-established poets, of course, can expect a much poorer deal. Be prepared to subsidize yourself. Whatever you do, establish a second string. Become an expert in something else.

12
Doing It Yourself

Writers imagine that they must be commercially published in order to be proud of their work. "If my manuscript is worthwhile, why didn't a commercial house accept it?" The myth persists.
Bill Henderson

You've tried all the usual channels and got nowhere. What can you do? Keep writing. You can do that, which at times will feel like massaging your head with rocks. Keep at it until you improve. Many good writers and quite a few great writers have found themselves in the same position — unaccepted, neglected, even ostracized — and a large number have then decided that the answer is to publish themselves. This doesn't have to be an act of vanity nor a sign of feeble writing. Self-publishing has a long and respectable tradition. It avoids the profit motive intervening in the role of poet — don't lose sight of the fact that successful publishers publish for profit, not for pleasure — and it allows you greater control.

The practice goes back a long way to the times when the publisher (the person who employs a printer to produce the books) and the bookseller (the distributor of the works) were often the same people. It was common for booksellers to be printers, quite usual for publishers to actually print their books themselves. Authors would subscribe their titles in advance — convince friends and acquaintances to pay for their copies before publication — and then when they'd covered enough, contract with a printer or bookseller to bring the edition out.

Robert Burns collected 350 advance subscribers to his *Poems, Chiefly in the Scottish Dialect* which he paid a Kilmarnock printer to produce in 1786. William Blake published his *Songs of Innocence* in 1789, doing everything except making the paper himself. Shelley, who self-published *The Necessity of Atheism* in 1811 using an Oxford printer, ran into considerable trouble when he found his subject matter too controversial for local booksellers, who refused to handle it. He pioneered a technique now common among small-press operators and many well known authors. Entering the premises of booksellers Munday and Slater while the principals were at lunch, he told the shop assistant all had been previously arranged and scattered copies of his book throughout the store. His undoing was to also build a display of the book in the shop's window. This was spotted by the local clergy, who complained vociferously and the offending books were removed and burned.

Do-it-yourself helped Byron, who successfully produced his collections *Fugitive Pieces* and *Poems on Various Occasions* before being taken up by a London publisher. Edgar Allan Poe, trying the same route, was less lucky: his *Tamerlane*, self-published in 1827, vanished without a trace. He'd managed, after some difficulty, to pay for a print run of forty copies, all of which were sent out for review. Unfortunately there was absolutely no response. Perhaps the greatest of all early self-publishers was Walt Whitman, who doggedly printed and reprinted succeeding editions of his *Leaves of Grass*, writing splendid reviews of the book himself and toting copies of it around the countryside in a basket. His tireless determination kept the book in print for decades. The final self-published edition came out in 1892, the year of his death.

A lot of self-publishing is done for the express purpose of getting the work spread out among friends and critics. Ezra Pound did this in 1907 with a one-hundred-copy run of *A Lume Spento*. Sometimes the act is engaged in because the poets think they can do it better than anyone else. This was the case with William Morris, whose edition of *Poems By the Way* is as much a work of art as a book as it is as verse. Often, though, self-publishing is used as a palliative for frustration. If nobody else is interested, then do it yourself. Advances in technology have made this both easy and cheap. Publishing is suddenly available for all.

Many contemporary writers engage in the practice. Some like Bob Cobbing and Ian Hamilton Finlay do it because they enjoy their self-created flexibility and produce the vast majority of their work this way. Others such as Michael Horovitz, John Brunner, Allen Fisher, Jon Silkin and Eric Mottram self-publish when it suits them — perhaps because their regular publishers are over-stretched or even actively dislike the new piece of work. Most important is speed. Doing it yourself means you can do it now. No waiting, no publisher's queues which can go on for years. The work appears with its paint still wet and for many that is an important consideration.

There are three levels of intensity to self-publishing and you'll need to decide which one you want to operate at before you proceed:

1. Do you want a small number of copes of your book simply to prove you can do it, perhaps enough to give away to friends? This isn't really economic publishing but if you can afford it you can pass the whole task to the printer of your choice and have it off your back.
2. Do you want enough copies to make it available locally, to have it on sale in the local bookshop and perhaps those of nearby towns?
3. Or do you want to tackle the big one — have the book widely available, perhaps nationally, certainly in most large towns?

Your decision will be affected by two things: how much money you've got available for the project and how much time you've got to spend.

If you've followed the chapter on the preparation of a book-length MS you will have your selected poems in order and you will also have found a title. You'll have now to think of a name for yourself as publisher. This isn't essential but it helps. If your name is John Jones you could call yourself John Jones Publishers. The John Jones I know did this when he published *Way Back to Ruthin*, his first book of verse. However you may like to invent a title — most people do: it somehow maintains the illusion of publication as distinct from just having the things printed yourself. Here are a few names taken at random from the current Association of Little Presses membership list: *Overdue Books*, *Pauper's Press*, *The Aulton Press* (from Aulton Croft where the owner lives), *BB Books* (from the press operator, Dave Cunliffe's postcode), *Moss Rose Press*, *Spineless Books*, *Unidentified Flying Printer*, *Prest Roots Press*, *Tiger Bay Books* (curiously not in Cardiff), *Re-Verb*, *Crabflower Pamphlets*, *Ada Press*, *Alun Books*, and *Maypole Editions*.

You'll also need what is known in the trade as an ISBN, an International Standard Book Number. This is a group of numbers that you'll find printed on almost all modern books, usually on the back cover and on the verso of the title page. They look like this — 0 85031 398 8. It helps booksellers and librarians in their ordering procedures and also facilitates computer stock control. They are free and can be allocated to every book; the first part of the number will be a special prefix identifying the publisher. Write or phone the Standard Book Numbering Agency, 12 Dyott Street, London WC1A 1DF (071 836 8911) — tell them your chosen press name, address, author's name, title of book and binding (at this stage in your career this will inevitably be paperback) and they'll send a number by return.

You can phone them if things are desperate but they prefer you to write. These numbers are not a legal obligation; if you don't want one, don't have one. However the agency, once it learns of your book, may allocate one nonetheless. The prime advantage of ISBNs, from the point of view of the self-publisher, is that they make your book more readily traceable. And that can mean orders, and sales and people reading your poems, and one imagines that this is what you want.

Formats for collections of poetry are not rigid but there are certain conventions and I'd advise following them until you are practised enough to diverge. A typical book will run like this:

(1) *Title-page* — name of book, name of poet, name of press.
(2) *Verso of title-page* (the back of the title page) — publication data, copyright details and other information.
(3) *Contents page*.
(4) *Acknowledgements* (references to any of the poems' previous publication in magazines).
(5) *Preface* or *Introduction*.
(6) *The poems themselves*.

This kind of detail is easily demonstrated, look at any recent book you have on your shelves. The only page which might cause confusion is the *verso of title-page*. Overleaf is a typical example. All the basic information on one page. Your address (it's amazing how many self-publishers leave this vital piece of information off), the date of publication and the copyright symbol © conforming the book to international conventions. You can put a lot of other stuff on the verso of the title-page if you wish — information about rights, dire warnings against copying by means mechanical, fair or foul, Library of Congress catalogue card numbers, etc. My example limits this to "All rights reserved", plus some data on the printer and an acknowledgement of financial help received. Much else can be useful but somehow pretentious on a poet's first slim self-published work.

If you took the decision I mentioned earlier — to go for national distribution — things will now really hot up. You'll have to see your bank to arrange a loan, because no matter what else you've got you are probably also going to need an advance from them. If you took one of the easier options it will still be expensive but perhaps not as bad.

It is impossible here to say how much a book costs to publish because there is no such thing as a standard book. It all depends

Watching For Dolphins

Copyright © David Constantine 1983
All rights reserved

ISBN: 0 906427 54 1

First published 1983 by
Bloodaxe Books Ltd,
P.O. Box 1SN,
Newcastle upon Tyne NE99 1SN.

Bloodaxe Books Ltd acknowledges
the financial assistance of Northern Arts.

Typesetting & cover printing by
Tyneside Free Press Workshop Ltd, Newcastle.

Printed in Great Britain by
Unwin Brothers Ltd, Old Woking, Surrey.

on how many pages you want, how many copies, which printing process you use and how you want the publication bound. This is the place where a lot of self-publishers overreach themselves. They make the wrong decision as to quantity or quality and the whole deal goes up the spout. I imagine there to be a good many houses up and down the country where the loft is stuffed with unsold copies of an overprinted book, or where the poet is downstairs wrapped in a blanket, having sold everything else to raise enough publishing capital and then through incorrect pricing failed to get it back.

Take it slowly. Go down to the library or, better, the bookshop; buy and study other people's books not for their content but for how they look. Find one that you like, where the design seems to work, and base your first on that.

13
Actually Doing It

For a moment let's imagine a typical poetry book, based on a few averages. It'll contain around 26 poems, mostly short, with only two or three continuing for more than 40 lines. There'll be no illustrations and the typesetting will be straightforward with no footnotes, prose sections or use of italic type. Such a book, by an apparently unknown poet, isn't going to sell very many copies, you might think. What would be the best quantity to print — 50 copies? 50,000? I've known poets come unstuck at both these extremes.

Choosing the print run

Usually British and Irish sales for a mainstream publisher with national distribution — say Faber and Faber, Hutchinson or Secker and Warburg — are quite low. With the exception of the drum banging which surrounds things like 40,000 sales of Larkin's *Collected Poems* publishers are extremely reluctant to pass out actual figures and if you ask the poets you'll find them just as cagey. But for the first collection, sales will be hundreds and rarely more. A lot depends on how pushy the poet is. Can he sell copies at poetry readings? Will she badger the local shop to take extra copies of a title by a "local" author? It is worth noting here that comparative sales figures for small presses and their commercial counterparts are similar — the mainstream publisher sells on reputation, the small press does it on personal contact. I would suggest that for someone without established connections in the publishing and book trades 300 copies is around the right number for a first self-published edition.

Book publishing prices are not constant throughout the printing run — the cost of each copy becomes significantly cheaper the more you print. The expensive part is known as origination — setting the whole book in type and putting it onto the machine. Once you have paid for the first one hundred then the price for doing an extra 250 will not be that much more. If you take this to its logical conclusion and print 5,000 you'll have the problem of selling them. The market, no matter how highly you prize your own capabilities as a poet, just will not be there.

Sit back for a moment and think of how many friends, relations, acquaintances you've got. Will they all buy a copy? Probably not. But this doesn't happen to Roger McGough, Ted Hughes or Patience Strong, you say; they sell books by the sinkful. You'd have to be well known to shift books like that. Are you? Can you be? Really? These are long shots. One in a million chances. Don't gamble on that happening, it won't. Put your money on a horse. (It is interesting to note here — as an aside — that many of the periodical and newspaper publishers who use the late Patience Strong's inspirational outpourings do not regard her as a poet. When I enquired as to what poetry they published they told me none.)

What printing method?

Your choice here really depends on the level of intensity you picked in the last chapter. Publishing as a hobby can be considerably more expensive than hi-fi; but it can be cost-cut. The more you can do yourself the cheaper it will be.

The process of bringing out a book splits readily into three:

(1) Writing the text and deciding in what order it should run.

(2) Setting that text in type of some sort — the *origination* already referred to.

(3) Running this off in multiple copies and putting these together to form a book.

You will already have done (1) and if that is as far as your creative ability goes then now is the time to approach a commercial printer. Nearly all the stock on the shelves of your average bookshop will have been produced that way and most of it by a system of printing known as *offset-litho*. Here the typeset matter — the text — is converted photographically into a printing plate and then impressed on the paper via a rotary machine. The older printing system where movable type is locked in a chase rather like a giant John Bull Printing Outfit and then pressed directly onto paper is known as *Letterpress*. It is now largely redundant. This was the system Caxton pioneered and the one which most people think of when they hear the word "print". It is still used by some specialists who prefer its undoubted quality, most notably the *private* presses producing expensive limited editions of books as examples of the printer's art.

Commercial applications however are extremely rare. Offset-litho is sleek, flexible, modern. If you go commercially it will be the system you'll use.

Take your sample book — the one on which you intend to base your own — round to a printer. Use Yellow Pages, try for a larger firm to begin with. Turn up and ask how much they'll charge to run (say) 300 copies of a book similar to the one in your hand. It will certainly amaze you how large a sum they'll quote — well out of all proportion to the final selling price you might have had in mind. If you are willing to subsidise your work to this extent then go ahead. Big commercial firms usually provide quality production. But do shop around. Quotations can vary wildly. Often the smaller company, more ready to deal in short runs, will quote you a more reasonable sum. But it will still be a lot.

All is not lost, however. The way to cut costs is to get involved yourself.

Setting your own text

This should be the first operation in any attempt to make things cheaper. Setting work in type is time consuming and therefore costly. Do it yourself and you will save a considerable sum. The aim here is to produce for the printer what is known as "camera ready copy" — the poems set in black type laid out on blank sheets of paper *exactly* as you would like to see them reproduced. From these the printer will make the plates.

Could you bear to have your work reproduced by typewriter? Hand-thumped Olympias with their often uneven lines and irregular letter shapes look pretty amateur but electric typers, especially daisy wheel models using once-only carbon ribbons, can be presentable enough.

Much better results can be obtained by resorting to the new technology, assuming of course that you have access. But beware, not everything is what it seems. Since the advent of the Amstrad PCW word processors have become pretty common household appliances. They manipulate text, shift it, delete it, cut and paste it, tidy its margins and check its spelling. But at the cheaper end they are not that hot at printing out. Most home machines come with what's known as a dot-matrix printer — fast but with results that are blurry to look at. Not much use to the self-publisher. Those which come with daisy wheel, ink-jet or even the much more expensive laser printer on the other hand most definitely are. Yet despite having part of their apparatus known as a *printer* these machines remain glorified typewriters. They produce text — once. For multiple copies you must still resort to other machines and inevitably a human printer.

A notable advance in word processing has been the development of Desk Top Publishing programs but these too are not what they seem. Desk Top Publishing (DTP) does not mean publishing in the traditional sense; rather it refers to "page make up", in simple terms the preparation on a monitor screen of text exactly as it is to appear on the printed page. This can range from the single poem adrift in a sea of blank space to DTP's speciality — multi-columnar text in multiple typefaces, headlined and complete with illustrations and footnotes. Once the operator is happy with what is on the screen the results are produced as camera ready copy on the laser printer.

Like word processing Desk Top Publishing is a system of copy preparation. The running of multiple copies — the rest of the traditional publishing process — still has to be done elsewhere.

A good half-way house in DIY typesetting is to put your text on a word processor and then pass the disk to a specialist setter who will produce typeset copy directly without the expensive need to retype. The keystrokes only need occur once. You would still have to paste up your own copy of course, but given a steady hand and a keen eye that is a relatively simple job.

Poets interested in trying out this aspect of self-publishing are advised to try a few dummy runs first. What you see is not always what you get. Suitable specialist setting companies can be found by talking to your printer, checking the small ads in the computer magazines or by contacting either the Association of Little Presses or the Small Press Group (see Appendix 1). Saxon Ltd of Heritage Gate, Derby DE1 1DD (0332 361370), produce a free booklet *Typesetting From Author's Disk — An Introduction To The New Technology*.

Producing the pages

Having set the text what next? The final step — running the pages off and binding them up. The best quality, least-hassle approach is to stick with the commercial printer but this can still cost. High Street instant print shops may prove competitive on very short runs but check. Better would be a community print shop if there is one in your area. These are usually attached to a school or college and involve actually handling the equipment yourself. This can be fun or not depending on your practical ability. Whatever else it would be an experience. Check evening class provision in your area. ALP can advise on London facilities.

Failing offset litho with its reliance on at least some technical knowledge the modern alternative is the photocopier. Things have come a long way from the almost illegible cloudy-grey of early Rank Xerox. Today it is often hard to tell copy from original — results are good. Contemporary copiers are fast, clean, offer spot colour (or total colour if you are willing to pay for it), enlargement and reduction facilities and are not really much more difficult to operate than a television set. Access is the problem. Commercial reproduction bureaux set up mainly to service local offices are pricey. Check, compare costs. You will be lucky indeed to find anyone charging less than 6p for a single A4 sheet. Avoid at all costs buying a £100 hot-paper copier of the kind found advertised in the newspaper classifieds and never go near the coin-in-the-slot machines found in colleges and public libraries.

To fully appreciate the advantages of the photocopier's flexibility and economic operation the dedicated self-publishing poet needs to approach the system unofficially by the back door; personally if possible or failing that through a friend.

Photocopying is not a system to be sneered at. Results can be surprisingly effective. Perhaps the best examples in this country come from that pioneer of alternative printing technologies, Bob Cobbing. Using a Canon NP4540 which he owns and running over 10,000 copies a month Cobbing has spent the past decade pushing photocopying to its limits — much as he did earlier with his Gestetner duplicator — turning small publishing into an art form. His press, *Writers Forum*, founded in the early 60s has produced more than 475 publications in editions of all shapes and sizes. If you intend to use a photocopier you might like to get hold of some Cobbing productions to see just what can be done. Write to him at 89a Petherton Road, London N5 2QT.

Cover

An important part — mass-market paperback publishers will tell you it is the most important part. A well designed, attractive cover will entice prospective buyers to pick your book up. Half the battle won.

Use a designer or artist to help you if you can. Consider colour although this will add to the cost. Print on gloss board at very least. Better is to have the printed result laminated to give it that shiny, expensive look. Even if you are running the entire book on a photocopier from typewriter-set originals this may well be the one place where you might benefit from professional help.

Collating and binding

You could pay for these processes to be done but again you'll save by doing some yourself.

Collating is the term for putting the pages together. It usually means walking round and round a table full of stacked sheets successively taking one from each pile. It's boring, it's very time consuming, and it's not even good for the soul. I once put together a 40-page, 400 copy edition of the poems of William Wantling in six hours, which gives an idea of how long it takes.

Binding the pages together and into the cover is simplest done by wire stapling. If you can borrow a heavy-duty, long-arm stapler it makes the task much easier. These machines are rentable from hire shops.

Perfect binding — books held into a squared spine by special glue — is not beyond the dedicated self-publisher. It takes time and a heap of house bricks to act as a press. Enquire at your art supplies shop about suitable glues.

Other Methods of Book Production

There was a time when almost everything not published professionally was part of the "mimeo revolution" — home produced by literary renegades on a duplicator and by today's standards ragged and ink-stained enough to be classed as illegible. You will be hard put now to find a spirit-duplicator anywhere outside the antique trade but the more conventional Gestetner and Roneo machines can still be found gathering dust at the back of offices or at bargain prices on the used equipment market. Hardly anyone uses them for publishing anymore but if you are prepared to persevere then reasonable results can be obtained. Check 70s vintage *Writers Forum* productions or the early output of Peter Hodgkiss's *Galloping Dog Press* (45 Salisbury Gardens, Newcastle-upon-Tyne NE2 1HP).

The best book on the subject is *Publish It Yourself And Make It Pay* by Ian Templeton (Pikers' Pad).

Before embarking on the project — if this is what you have now determined to do — you should read up a little more on printing. It is not necessary to be technically knowledgeable but print is more than letters and ink. You'll find a list of recommended titles in Appendix 4. These books are not complex and won't take you weeks to read but they will illuminate. Since the project is going to cost you money, don't cut corners. Learn all you can.

Beyond the book

Before I move on to talk about what to do with your collection once it is printed, it might be worth considering, briefly, a few alternatives to the book itself. Despite the arrival of the paperless society and the relentless and all embracing rise of television, sales of traditionally produced books have gone up not down. Nonetheless recent advances in technology have made it possible for some non-book alternatives to come to the fore.

Poets whose work involves performance, sound-text experimentation or who are simply good readers will have already come up against the limitations of print and will have turned to the audio cassette. Done on a home basis it is inexpensive and, unlike print, has a unit cost which remains constant throughout the run. You can record your "master" on a good quality domestic recorder, preferably using metal tape, and then either use a twin-deck machine to make copies according to demand or employ a cassette duplicating company to run multiples in advance. Andrew Brown of *Tak Tak Tak* in Leeds uses Professional Magnetics Ltd, Cassette House, 329 Hunslet Road, Leeds, LS10 1NJ (tel: 0532 706066). *Tak Tak Tak* is an irregular magazine with accompanying cassette featuring music, poetry and verbal experimentation. In the early days blank C40s were purchased in bulk and reproduced domestically but with circulation rising the pain of listening to the same thing 200 times became too hard to bear. *Tak Tak Tak* now let Professional Magnetics do the whole job.

Packaging for comparatively small quantities of tapes can be expensive if you stick with the professionals. *Tak Tak Tak* use standard cassette cases but with their own typewriter produced labels and photocopied inserts. Eric Vonna-Michell's classic *Balsam Flex* tapes came inside hand-labelled wedding cake boxes which made an exact fit.

Some self-publishers have experimented with microfiche — a convenient form of microfilming where up to 270 sheets of text are reduced to the size of a postcard. To read them you need a viewer. You may have seen these TV-like readers in bookshops and libraries. Both Bill Griffiths with his *Pyrofiche* and Chris Jones with *Jones Family Editions* have in the past used the medium for poetry but today no longer do so. The seemingly unresolvable difficulty which both found unsurmountable was the dearth of viewers among their potential audience. That and the fact that you can't really read a microfiche in bed. The medium remains the domain of directory publishers and academic presses.

Computers offer better possibilities. Already in common use everywhere as information storage, manipulation and retrieval devices and often worked creatively by poets it was inevitable that before too long someone would produce a genuine poetry magazine on disk. Ed Jewasinski's *Agog Ago Go* runs on the BBC for home users and has a visual version for those with access to an IBM PC or clone. It's an interactive mag with plenty of opportunity for the reader to join in and if you want a hard copy you run one on your printer. *Agog Ago Go*, 116 Eswyn Road, Tooting, London SW17 8TN.

If writing rather than publication is your problem then you might consider Ansible Information's *A.I.Q.* program for the Amstrad which actually produces random and seemingly unending verse before your eyes. Delving into a number of pre-prepared lists of words and phrases called "lexicons" it reads, shuffles what it finds and prints the results structured as poetry. Nothing can be predicted and the fun starts when the poet abandons the prepared word lists and sets up his or her own. A commercial application of this idea is the *Computer Poet*, a machine which with the input of the customer's name and town of residence prints personalised doggerel inside greetings cards. As verse it is dreadful but as a gimmick it sells. Would Caxton see any of this as poetry or even publication? Hard to tell.

And the future? The CD is already in use as a data store. If you are that interested the Post Office will sell you one containing every UK address and postcode. Future books viewable on palm-sized LCD flat-screens are on the way. For the present these remain formidably expensive but keep your eyes open — the perpetual pre-eminence of paper is no longer a certain thing.

14
What Do You Do With It Next?

If you've got this far, you must be serious. Your book is printed and the copies are all sitting in your front room. The first thing you'll have noticed is that they don't look as many as expected. You imagined, perhaps, a room full and it turns out you can hide them all under the table. Don't be deceived. There are plenty there. Pick up the stacks or packets carefully — paper weighs a lot.

Deciding the retail price

You'll need to work out a selling price. This can be done following commercial principles — find the unit cost and multiply by three. One to cover your print costs, one to cover distribution (that's the discount shops will require), and one to share between overheads and profit for yourself. On the other hand you may only be concerned to get your work around and feel that if you get some of your investment back that's a bonus. It's important to look at what other people charge for their books — check at your bookshop. Don't just pick one title, look at a group, take an average. If your selling price is significantly greater, then no matter how much it costs you to produce, your book is not going to move. These are market forces; only ignore them if you are operating where there are no shops — and even then people will make poor comparison between what you offer and what they can get mail order.

- Decide your price.
- Pitch it correctly for the look, style, and size of your book.
- Allow for bookshop discounts — a third.
- Stick to it.

You might as well acknowledge that people don't buy much poetry, they don't read it. Once your book is in the shops it will most probably just sit there. It won't go like hot cakes; poetry books never do. But don't let us be too defeatist. There must be some market.

You've had it printed. Stick to your guns.

A lot of what you do now depends on how far you want to go and whether or not you are concerned to recover the money you've put in. A lot of poets are content simply to circulate their books among friends. It satisfies vanity without using a vanity publisher. It proves you can do it. It prepares you for the next step — the magazine appearance you haven't managed or the acceptance of your next collection by a commercial press. There is a lot in this; once you've done something, published a small book, it makes you more credible. You've proved your determination and seriousness. There is no guarantee, but at least you'll have given yourself a better chance.

Copyright libraries

Whatever you decide, you have certain obligations under the Copyright Act of 1911. These are nothing to do with any "registering" of copyright (see Chapter 10), but are legal requirements to deposit six copies of your book *free of charge* in the following places:

1. The British Library, Legal Deposit Office, Boston Spa, Wetherby, W.Yorkshire L523 7BY.
2. The Bodleian Library, Oxford.
3. The Library of Cambridge University.
4. The Library of Trinity College, Dublin.
5. The National Library of Scotland.
6. The National Library of Wales.

The British Library copies should be sent direct, the others in one packet, care of the Agent for the Libraries, A.T. Smail, 100 Euston Street, London, NW1 2HQ. Do not include any correspondence, merely a note to the British Library indicating your selling price. Many publishers object to this obligatory "freebie" of six copies of every book they publish, yet the aims of the requiring Act are quite altruistic. It is to establish, among other things, publicly accessible depositories of everything in print. The problem today is not the depositing of copies but the eventual arrival of those books on the libraries shelves. There is a log jam and not enough money in the library system to see it through. Not that you have a choice, however; if you fail to send copies then the Libraries can take you to court.

Don't think that once you've got your book and handled the legal requirements that you can sit back and let a distributor do the rest for you. Big national distributors such as Hammicks or Heathcote won't deal with small presses and that much-discussed animal *the small and private press distributor* still doesn't exist. Selling (i.e. distribution of) a book is as hard as printing it. And, as you'll have found out if you did most of the work yourself, printing can be as wearing as writing. The battle is not over yet.

Organizing the sales campaign

The first steps in your sales campaign could be as follows.

1.   *Review Copies*. Send these to the local newspaper, television and radio stations and to any literary magazines which you've seen reviewing small-press books or which you feel may give you a favourable report or indeed any report at all. If a lot of your poems are about a particular subject, cars for example, you could send a review copy to one of the motoring magazines. With the local media copies enclose a "press release" telling the story of how you came to publish it yourself and a bit about what else you do — something they could base a "local inhabitant makes good" story on. If you know the names of any programme presenters, producers or journalists then mark your package for their attention.

A few days after mailing, ring up the more important local outlets and ask if your book has arrived. If the response is affirmative ask if they intend carrying a story. If, however, they don't appear to know anything about your poems — and this is the more likely response — ask if they'd like another copy and at the same time ask the name of someone to whom it should be sent. The object here is to generate *free* coverage of your book locally, which will promote sales, and not necessarily critical response. You are news because you have done it yourself, not because you are a great poet. Do not in any circumstance contact literary magazines this way. They'll review your book if they choose to, but it takes time — a year is not unusual, six months about par for the course. Do not be disappointed if like Edgar Allan Poe you get no reviews at all. Hundreds of new poetry collections come out every year — very few are awarded the honour of being reviewed.

2.   *Don't be talked into buying advertising space* in newspapers or anywhere else. It might sound a good idea, somehow legitimizing

you as a publisher, but remember that even the big publishers rarely do it, unless it's for a special book or a touchy author. At your level of operation it is likely to be a complete waste of cash.

3. *Go round your local bookshops* — all of them, the chains, the independents, the market stalls — and the ones in nearby towns as well. Include corner newsagents and perhaps record shops. Show them the book — tell them of your forthcoming publicity if you've succeeded with the media, allude to its probability if you have not. They'll take copies from you — maybe six or a dozen — and ask for trade terms, usually specifying "sale or return". This means paying you later for copies they've sold and at the same time, returning any which remain. A variation is "see-safe", which means the shop pays you on receipt of the books but requires you to take back for credit any copies with which they are subsequently stuck. Buy a cheap duplicate-invoice pad and record details of all transactions, leaving a copy with your books at the shop. Occasionally shops will pay outright, which saves trouble, otherwise give them a few weeks — six would be best — before you pester them for your dues. Expect to have to do this in most shops; you are a very small account, they'll probably pay you last. Accepted trade terms in this field are 33% discount for firm sales, 25% for single copies, 25% for sale or return and in all cases the publisher bears the cost of any postage which might be involved.

The standard "dirty-tricks" for selling to shops are as follows: go round the day after your visit and remove your books from the shelf where the bookshop assistant has apparently hidden them and reposition them prominently on one of the shop's in-store displays. No doubt someone will eventually spot this and move them back again but at least they'll have been right in the public gaze for a while. This happens in the shop I manage all the time and although I resented it at first I've learned to regard these promotion-conscious poets (and they are usually poets) as part of the trade's vitality. The second device is to ring up asking if the book is in stock or to send a friend in to buy a copy. If it does nothing else, this will draw the shop staff's attention to your book being on their shelves. A self-publisher I know found the local shop selling out as fast as he could deliver copies and concluded that he'd somehow hit the big one. Investigation showed that actually his girl-friend had bought most of them without saying. She'd found that high sales boosted self-regard and as a consequence his ardour improved.

4. *Indulge in direct selling.* This is more profitable as the bookshop's one-third discount becomes your own. If you've a number of willing friends you could perhaps convince them to help by doing the same thing. Go round all your acquaintances, avoiding no one. For this to work you'll have to tackle them all. Carry a bag of books, exaggerate your difficulties. Tell them the sob-story about being unable to give away copies as often as you'd like because of your investment etc., etc. It's amazing how many friends will at first expect a free copy. When they put their hands in their pockets — take the money and run. If you feel bolder than this, sell to strangers on the street. Stand outside your local library and stop people. Be prepared for abuse. Avoid selling in pubs; I did this and had beer thrown over me for being (a) a nuisance, (b) not as good as Wordsworth and (c) a nancy for writing poetry in the first place. Selling your book further afield than this is difficult. You can visit other towns for the day and blitz their bookshops certainly, but they may only have one, and it can be expensive and very time-consuming. If you are determined or have ignored earlier advice and have printed so many thousand copies that you must, then the following points may be of help:

● Telephone selling. Ring up all the bookshops you can find the telephone numbers for. Do this mid-morning or mid-afternoon on weekdays. Avoid Saturdays. Ask for the buyer, say you represent Whammo Books or whatever name you've chosen. Keep your voice steady. Do not own up to actually being the author concerned but suggest that your press has published the best book of new poems this year and that they might like to take copies. Offer sale or return terms *loudly* if they sound resistant; remind them that they are running no financial risk by ordering. Be pleasant. They will usually offer to order a few copies just to get you off the phone. If they say they'll order from you through the post, they are lying; they won't. Get a confirmed order there and then, ask for an order number. Persist. It's like buying religious magazines, in the end they'll accept just to make you go away. I once knew a perfectly terrible poet who sold hundreds of copies this way. His phone bills were high but he'd built an allowance for that into the retail price of his book. In two weeks he'd talked to nearly every big bookshop in the country and secured orders by the heap.

● Join the Association of Little Presses (ALP). Membership is currently £10. Send to 89a Petherton Road, London N5 2QT.

Formed in 1966 as a pressure group to better the lot of independent and mainly literary publishers, the ALP now offers a considerable bargain in exchange for your membership fee. It produces a newsletter of information for small publishers, an annual directory-cum-catalogue of members' publications and offers a telephone advice service (071-226 2657) on most aspects of small-scale and self-publishing. Regularly there are ALP bookfairs (which sell members' books) and exhibitions (which show them off). Participate. You'll meet others and learn how they do it. You'll even sell a few books.

The Small Press Group of Britain is a similar organisation, although of much more recent origin. Membership here costs £12. Send to BM Bozo, London WC1N 3XX.

● Advertise in *The Bookseller* (journal of the book trade) classifieds — 12 Dyott Street, London WC1 — for a freelance representative to carry your book on commission. It's a long shot, but it may come off. This means an independent traveller who visits many bookshops and carries a broad range of titles may also be convinced to show potential buyers yours. If the rep gets any orders he or she will pass these on for you to fulfil (i.e. deliver and invoice), and in return will expect a commission, 10 per cent or more of invoice value, on completed transactions.

You can read further about sales in my *How To Publish Yourself* (see Appendix 3), which covers a fair amount of what you will need to know.

Publishing is what the exercise has been all about, of course. You've done it. It's out. You'll have satiated whatever demand it was which made you begin, now you can sit back. Curiously, though, it doesn't work like that. The poet is never satisfied by achievement, at least not for long. If you've published once, you'll have to do it again. And after that to prove it was no fluke once more, and so it goes.

As a spin-off you may have found that you actually enjoy the process of having things printed. This is how many a small press begins. Use your blossoming expertise, print others whose work you like, poets who are in the same unpublished state that you once were. You may also, now that you've achieved something, consider approaching the Arts Council of Great Britain (in Wales the Welsh Arts Council, in Scotland the Scottish Arts Council, in Northern Ireland the Northern Irish Arts Council) or if you live in the Republic of Ireland the Arts Council An Chomhairle Ealaíon, Ireland or your

Regional Arts Association for help (see Appendix 2 for details of addresses). All of these organizations support small publishers financially, although the degree of support varies from area to area. Generally speaking, hard cash aid towards the cost of publishing little-known poets is difficult to obtain and is almost never given to self-publishers bringing out their first work. However if you've published one book on your own and wish to continue there is no harm in asking. Some Arts Associations offer help with distribution, often by buying bulk copies from you and retailing them via special bookstands set up in selected shops, arts centres and libraries throughout their region. Others will review and advertise your work in their magazines and newsheets. All should be able to offer advice on the art of small publishing itself.

15

Vanity Presses

POEMS WANTED. Publisher seeks new material for forthcoming anthology.

POETS, seeking publication? Go no further. Send examples of your work.

ESTABLISHED PUBLISHER seeks material for new poetry anthology.

WANTED. New Poetry for *Crown of the Muse*. Prestigious anthology. National circulation.

WRITERS. Publish your poetry with us. Experienced publisher continually looking for new material.

These are the kind of advertisements you may regularly see in the personal columns of local newspapers, Sunday weeklies and the classified sections of magazines. All those of you who've been involved in poetry publishing for any length of time will know them to be nonsense. No one ever need *advertise* for poems, the market is permanently flooded. Editors keep their heads down, hoping the next sack of mail is not really for them.

These publishers are the *vanity presses*. Their names change, they move about. They are after your money. They have no concern for literature at all. It may come as a surprise to some poets to suddenly be asked to pay to have their work published but for others, unfortunately, it has become the accepted thing. Vanity presses are so called because they prey on the "vanity" of writers — usually poets because there are more of them to the mile — people who can be persuaded to part with money in exchange for seeing themselves in print.

The presses themselves insist there is nothing wrong with this. They provide a service, there is a need. They even admit that some of the works they bring out are so awful, so absolutely devoid of any worth at all, that their method is the only possible way in which publication could occur. The poets pay, the vanity presses deliver the goods.

The element of conning becomes apparent when you study their reaction to submitted work. To begin with, vanity presses have absolutely no standards and indeed would publish a shuffled telephone directory or a gas bill if someone paid them. They accept all they are sent. Poets get letters telling them how good their work is. "Meticulously crafted", "splendid writing", "first-class work", and suchlike, when in fact the verse has not been read *at all*. The response will, in the flow of its false praise, mention that in this time of rising printing costs a charge of £15 or £30 or whatever has, regrettably, to be made to each contributing poet. This will help defray costs. The charge is always described as modest although it almost never is. It is mentioned as an afterthought and the poet, so blinded by the thrill of acceptance, rushes out and pays. Some only stop to consider what has occurred when the cheque has gone. Most remain quite happy, thinking that this is how it is always done.

The vanity presses claim to have sound literary judgement and to use this for the benefit of their writers. This is blatantly untrue. Bernard Braden in his days as a television consumer-watchdog arranged for three poems to be submitted, pseudonymously, to a vanity press. One was a piece of Wordsworth, one the doodlings of a seven-year-old and the third a cut-up of the evening newspaper. All three were accepted. "Your work shows great creativity," came the reply, "we intend including it all in our next anthology, *Star Gem Poems of the Decade*. Please send £30."

If poets continue to accept this kind of exploitation as an authentic assessment of what they are doing they will never stand a chance of improving. Praise a feeble poem and the next poem is liable to be feeble too.

Additionally the vanity presses purposely complicate things in order to impress. Their ubiquitous acceptance letters are accompanied by wordy contracts and permission forms which actually have little standing but give the impression that great things are going on. The whole operation is a thicket of unfulfillable promise designed to pull you in, emptying your pockets as you come. You may order the great anthology *in advance* at a special rate (no such things as contributor's free copies, of course), you can buy extra copies for your friends, you can have it leather bound and then for a further fee have your name gold-blocked on the cover — *Golden Meanderings of the Muse*: Jim Smith. Inside will be a contents page listing 300 other Smiths, their poems jammed in ten to the page. Why worry about legibility — who reads them anyway?

Part of the enticement to participate is an impressive list of national magazines and newspapers to which, it is claimed, review copies are sent. "We send copies of our anthologies to *The Sun*, *The Star*, *The Express*, *The Daily Mirror*, *Woman's Own*, *Woman*, *The News of the World . . .*" ran one recently (all, places incidentally, which do not review poetry at all). Conventional literary journals never, in my experience, ever mention vanity-press anthologies, let alone review them. The gap in their respective standards would make any comment meaningless. Booksellers, despite claims to the contrary, never stock vanity publications. They know the publishers for what they are and avoid them as a matter of course.

Who buys them? Libraries? No. The contributors, and perhaps their friends. It is where the title "vanity" comes from. The trap, once sprung, can be for much more than a few pounds. You submit again, spend more, they tell you that you are so good you should really have a book out. Have you got 30 poems? You send them in.

The book, naturally, will cost an arm and a leg — far more than if you'd gone directly to a printer and published it yourself. But you don't know this. You will recoup these costs in royalties, say their enticements. You agree, and of course the royalties never come. You'll have a contract in which the press agrees to print the 500 or so copies you'll pay for, but if you look closely you'll see that there is no mention of binding. Only those you've actually sold in advance are made up into books. The rest remain flat, uncut, and after a few years when you've forgotten about them get sold for pulp.

It is a mire, on the edges of legality, full of box numbers, accommodation addresses, telephone-answering machines and back-street printers. Edward Uhlan, the owner of America's largest vanity operation, Exposition Press, tells the whole tale in his self-published *The Rogue of Publisher's Row*. This is a kind of confession story, full of small-time racketeers who sell and resell mailing lists containing the names of thousands of likely poets. Uhlan is quite unrepentant. His original poetry operation, which he called the Adastra Publishing Company and ran under the pseudonym of Igor Ulianow ("feeling this name would be more to the taste of the recherché clientele"), published anybody, as long as they paid.

> In such a matter ethics and honesty are synonymous: people were willing to pay me for a specified service, and if I performed that service to their satisfaction the profits were deserved.

At one point he describes the buying of a 75,000-strong mailing list from a "song-shark publisher" — presumably in order to fleece the lyricist punters even further by selling them space for their worthless poems in his anthologies. "Song-sharks" are a vanity-fed variation on simple poetry publishing. They advertise claiming to be music publishers hunting for new lyrics:

> *Set Your Poetry To Music*. Our experienced song-writers require new lyrics for their next hit songs . . .

Needless to say, participation costs a fortune and the result is just as pointless an achievement as being published in *Diadems of the Muse* or its equivalent. For £100 you get a badly recorded tape of banal piano music with your poems garbled on top. An embarrassment to listen to rather than a Tin-Pan Alley success.

Vanity presses can be disastrous for your career prospects too. Many a novice has referred proudly to bought publication, imagining it to enhance his standing. In the places where reputations count, however, it always has the reverse effect.

The practice is insidious. It catches writers from across the spectrum — pensioners, housewives, teenagers, poets who have learned and now know better.

The advice is: *never pay, no matter how tempting the offer.*

The one possible exception is the variant known as subsidy publishing. This practice, more prevalent in the USA than here, occurs where regular publishers agree to bring out your book as long as you pay the shortfall in their estimates. You pay, but it is a real charge and not an exploitation. BE WARY — vanity presses, fearful of fraud, sometimes refer to themselves as subsidy publishers: "Authors wanted. We require poems. Acceptable work published on a subsidy basis." this implies both literary judgement and a sharing of costs. Actually the only poems unacceptable would be the libellous and the overtly licentious and the word *subsidy* certainly means paying well over the real cost.

For many years the main genuine exponent of subsidy publishing in Britain was the late Howard Sergeant's *Outposts*. The poets paid for their booklets but were not, on Sergeant's considerable reputation, ever exploited. They received the entire print run of a few hundred copies to sell and help recoup their outlay. Some now quite respectable names began their publishing careers like this: Alan Sillitoe, Ruth Fainlight, D.M. Black, Kevin Crossley-Holland, D.M. Thomas, Peter Jay, Harry Guest, Tom Earley, John Mole, Molly Holden, Peter Reading.

Today there are a number of small publishers treading these difficult waters, all vehement in their support for the cause of poetry as they see it, but all still asking for considerable financial support.

Make your choice. If you see an advertisement asking for poetry, ignore it. If you get an offer which involves you parting with money, turn it down. If you find it irresistible, *check first* the credentials of the people you are dealing with. Ask the Poetry Society, the Regional Arts Association, the Book Trust. Literary success ultimately rests on merit, not on how much you are able to pay.

16
Publishing Abroad

Why stick to your own back yard? There are many more markets for English-language poetry than just Britain and Ireland — India, South Africa, the Antipodes, Hong Kong, all of North America. In practice there is little point in sending a whole MS to these places — it's too costly, too distant, it takes too much time. There is no tradition, either, of new British or Irish poets getting their first books out abroad; foreign publishers have enough to worry about looking after their own. But poems in periodicals are different — and there are literally thousands of periodicals.

Don't get the idea that publication in distant parts will suddenly change you, make you a poet of international standing overnight. Rather it will show you just how large the field is and how completely insignificant your part. It is possible to be published in 300 magazines and still be considered unknown. Nonetheless it can be exciting, different, and something like *Poetry Chicago* always looks good on your c.v.

Foreign magazines are as open to British contributors as they are to contributors from anywhere else. Some may restrict themselves geographically as, for example, *Poetry Wales* does in Great Britain, but generally it's the poetry and not your address that will count. In the USA, British poets have a reputation for being rather dull, so send your liveliest work. You are competing for space the same as everyone else. The only difference is that you are at the end of an expensive postal chain and the local contributors are not.

The North American market is perhaps the biggest and most diverse anywhere. There are magazines devoted to just about every conceivable speciality and operating at all the levels there are of competence and ability to recognize ability. These range from the distinctly *non*-little magazines, like *Atlantic Monthly* (circulation 340,000) and the *New Yorker*, to 500-copy literary rockets like the *Greensboro Review* and *Blue Cloud Quarterly*. Sandwiched between the two extremes are the university-sponsored academic "heavies". US colleges competing among themselves for prestige often finance lavish academic magazines. These can run to hundreds of pages and have no real parallel in the UK. Examples are the *Kenyon Review* from Kenyon college, the University of Oregon's *Northwest Review*, *Prairie Schooner* from the University of Nebraska.

Competition is fierce at the top where payments are large. *Atlantic Monthly* is sent 77,000 poems a year, from which it publishes 40. The *New Yorker* receives, amazingly, 156,000 and manages to use 150. The regular market, however, is quite approachable and a large number of British and Irish poets have successfully placed their work there. Leading US magazines include *The American Poetry Review*, *Poetry*, *Crazy Horse*, *Antaeus*, *New England Review*, *The Antioch Review*, *North Dakota Quarterly*, *Sulfur*, *TriQuarterly*, *Unmuzzled Ox*, *Seneca Review*, *Georgia Review*, *Poetry East*, *The Painted Bride Quarterly*, *New York Quarterly*, *Salmagundi*, etc. While the Canadian market — which by now is fighting a rearguard action to maintain its independence from the USA — includes *Fiddlehead*, *Dalhousie Review*, *The Capilano Review*, *Antigonish Review*, *The Malahat Review*, *Poetry Canada Review*, *The Raddle Moon*, *Prairie Fire*, *Prism International*, *Quarry*, *Zymergy*, *The Plowman*, etc.

The other English-language markets are much smaller and in some ways more congenial than America. Neither *Going Down Swinging* (Australia) nor *Landfall* (New Zealand) have that contrived artiness to them which mars many an American magazine. Such markets often specifically seek British verse. Magazines include *Hermes*, *Ling*, *Meanjin Quarterly*, *Phoneix Review*, *Westerly*, *Poetry*, *Australia*, *Scripsi*, *Mattoid*, *Scarp*, *Kangaroo* (Australia), *Landfall*, *Unfold* (New Zealand), *Prakalpana*, *Swakal* (India), *Poetry* (Hong Kong), *The New Voices* (Trinidad), *Upstream* (RSA), *Kuk-Over-Al* (Guyana), *Voices Israel* (Israel), *Poetry Kanto*, *Poetry Nippon* (Japan), *2Plus2* (Switzerland) and there are many more.

Submission abroad is costly — phenomenally so when you compare it to sending inland. The weight stages are finer and each extra poem can cost you more. Learn to be selective. Discipline yourself to be short. When submitting remember the following:

1.   British stamps have no value overseas. Use IRCs — International Reply Coupons — obtainable at British post offices and exchangeable abroad for local stamps. One will get you a reply by sea, two will cover air mail.

2.   Poems can be sent either by air — which is expensive — or by sea mail, which is less so but can take months to reach somewhere like Australia. Costs can be reduced by using

Printed matter rates, which are roughly half standard charges and apply both to sea and air. Certain conditions must be met, however:

— Envelopes must be left unsealed, with the flap tucked in, and should be marked PRINTED MATTER in their top left corner.
— There must be no enclosure — no letter — just a slip with your name and address, the IRCs, and the return envelope.
— MSS must be *photocopies*. Carbons or typed originals are unacceptable. This may sound curious but it is a by-product of the necessity to allow all mechanically produced copy to travel as print.

3. Put *Great Britain* at the end of your address (if appropriate) and avoid UK, as Americans tend not to understand it. If you end your address with something like *Wales*, expect foreigners to embarrass you by adding *England*.

4. Use air-mail paper if you have to send originals or carbons and try air mail envelopes — they weigh significantly less.

It is much harder to study the products of a foreign market. The magazines are difficult to get hold of, difficult to judge. Some can be bought through the specialist bookshops listed in Appendix 1 or sample copies can be purchased directly, sometimes at reduced rates. You can send money abroad via your bank (which can be troublesome), via Visa, Mastercard, American Express or other credit cards if the recipients are capable of accepting payment in this form, by using a post office international money order, or if it is a very small sum involved some magazines are willing to accept payment in the form of multiple IRCs.

Names and addresses of foreign poetry outlets can usually be found in the "publications received" sections of many British little magazines as well as in PALPI (see Chapter 6 for details). The best sources, however, are clearly Judson Jerome's *Poet's Market* which has some 1,700 listings of mainly American markets, Len Fulton's *Directory of Poetry Publishers* with more than 2,000 entries (see Chapter 6 for details) as well as James Deahl's *Poetry Markets For Canadians* (League of Canadian Poets, 24 Ryerson Avenue, Toronto, Ontario M5T 2P3, Canada) which in addition to a thorough analysis of the local market suggests the best outlets for verse in English worldwide. All three directories give details of titles, address, size, frequency, circulation, cost, printing method, date of founding, together with a few lines of description including editorial preferences and in the case of Judson Jerome's huge enterprise examples of recent poetry published as well. Those with an eye on Ireland might like to look at *The Salmon Guide To Poetry Publishing in Ireland* which gives a similar overview of activity both North and South of the border (Salmon Publishing, Auburn, Upper Fairhill, Galway, Ireland).

17
Competitions

Competitions are where the "true bards are sorted from the vagabonds". or so some say. In Celtic Britain the post of bard was a real job at the royal courts. You could earn your living at it. The poets arranged contests, ostensibly to refine their art but actually to keep out the impostor and the incompetent. The tradition lives on in Wales, where annual Eisteddfods bestow small sums and great honour on successful bards.

Most contemporary poets, however, are more likely to be interested in money prizes of the kind offered in recent national competitions. Some of these have been blockbusters too, with four-figure sums awarded. Winning must be like coming up on the pools but with recognition taking the place of chance. The idea of the poetry competition appeals to many. Your entry is anonymous, the entry fee is small — at most a few pounds — and the prizes are glittering. If you lose, no one knows; it isn't public, there is no stigma to your failure — in fact you can argue that it isn't a failure at all.

There is a broadly held belief that poetry in this country is run by a literary mafia and unless your entreé into that group has been pre-ordained then you don't stand a chance. The pseudonymous poetry competition is a way of avoiding such a stricture. You and (for all anyone knows) Adrian Mitchell, John Stallworthy, Elizabeth Jennings and Lord Gowrie get your MSS into the same pile. This is then judged by the likes of Ted Hughes, who reads and supposedly makes his selection according to *merit* and not on the poet's name. The idea appeals widely — some competitions get tens of thousands of entries — and this is borne out by the often odd-sounding list of winners — complete unknowns with perhaps a minor poet appearing as a runner-up just to strengthen the democratic nature of the exercise. It is perfectly valid way of considering competitions. They are lotteries but ones in which ability does play a part.

The two major competitions of recent time — the *National Poetry Competition* run by the Poetry Society and the *Arvon Foundation* competition, run at first with the *Observer* and later Sotheby's — have attracted so many entries that a boom has resulted. A host of smaller prizefights, ranging from the Oriel posterpoem competition (prize £50 and publication of the winner as a poster) to the Bridport Arts Centre writing competition (£500 for a poem of not more than 40 lines), have sprung up often with the specific intention of raising cash. Not that the idea is new, either: literary competitions have always been around. It is the scale that has changed. Once a five-shilling booktoken and publication in the society newsletter was sufficient, now it has to be at least hundreds to ensure the competition's success. The bubble will burst when saturation point is reached and contests start to lose rather than make. For the moment, however, national and local organizers are still attracted to the idea and new trials of metrical strength continue to be announced in the literary magazines.

Some competitions are for single poems, some for whole collections, with book publication as part of the prize. Others are for verse on a specific theme or in a particular style, and this can often stimulate the apprentice poet. The entries are usually judged by a panel who do actually have to *read* all the poems, as participants have told me. They are first narrowed, rejecting the obvious, to a short list. Then after debate and dissent (this is good for those not placed) they become a list of winners. The result is almost always bland. As Gavin Ewart remarks, "When two or three poets judge other poets' work it is usually the solemn and unexceptionable that wins through." This is the competition poem — a middle-of-the-road, straight-up-and-down, no-risks piece which, with a lot of practice, can be made to win and then another one like it, time after time. Some poets are adept at it. Look through the lists of winners; the same names crop up again and again.

Well-known poets are sceptical of the value of competitions. They are regarded as exploitation and within the trade distrusted and often disliked. When canvassed for their attitudes to poetry competitions I found many poets disarmingly honest in their reply:

"I don't want to be placed 57th" — Fleur Adcock.

"I don't enter because I may not win" — Dannie Abse.

"I have entered. Wasn't placed. Don't like losing" — Adrian Mitchell.

Edwin Morgan, however, trusted his luck: "I did enter the Cheltenham Festival Comp a few years back — anonymously — and won a prize. The organizers asked some published poets to enter to 'keep standards up'."

Tillie Olsen in her book *Silences* is completely opposed to the idea of writers competing:

89

The sense of writers being pitted against each other is bred primarily by the workings of the commercial marketplace and by critics lauding one writer at the expense of another, while ignoring the existence of nearly all.

Take up your position and stick to it. No one will know what that is, of course, unless you happen to be one of the few who wins.

Before entering a competition and chucking away the fee (and I know generally this isn't much but you could give it to the blind), do consider the following:

— *Will winning, or indeed even rating a meritorious mention, add to your status*? You must be entering to further your career as a poet; if it was for the money you'd get better odds on the football pools. Is the competition known and respected — like the Cheltenham Festival Competition — or is it a much more local affair not worth remarking on in your c.v.?

— *Is there publication attached to the prize*? Such contests are always worth trying. Many publish a book of winning entries, often including runners up. If the competition is for a book of unpublished poems — as with some of the Arts Council and Regional Arts Association competitions — winning will mean a lot of attention, reviews and consequent sales for a collection which might otherwise have got little notice, if in fact it got published at all.

— *Is there an adjudicator's report*? Will you obtain any critical reaction to your work? Bearing in mind how hard such information is to obtain this may in itself be a reason for entering.

— *Finally, are the judges poets you respect or poets you're not keen on*? Perhaps there are even non-poets judging, people with no literary status but simply individuals who "know what they like". Would you be happy with their selections? If you've any doubts don't enter.

Awards

Poetry awards which are made for already published work are often confused with competitions. Prizes like the Commonwealth Poetry Prize, the Geoffrey Faber Memorial Prize, and the Signal Poetry Award are made each year and it is prudent to remind your publisher, if you have one, to send the organizers a copy of your book. Many of the Arts Councils and the Regional Arts Associations also make valuable book awards of various sorts which often result in considerable local prestige.

It is also possible to approach the Arts Councils, some Regional Arts Associations and the E.C. Gregory Trust Fund (which is administered by the Society of Authors, 84 Drayton Gardens, London SW10 95D) for financial assistance to allow yourself more time to write. These monies, sometimes known as bursaries, are a direct grant to the poet, rather than a prize. There is an obligation attached to them: recipients are expected to spend some specified time working on a particular project. You can't use the money for a holiday. Certain awards, fellowships or residencies will involve an amount of teaching, public readings or lectures. Others require the recipient to complete an identifiable body of work. Very few, if any, have no strings attached. The catch-22 is that bursaries are almost invariably made to poets with something to show — a book published or at very least considerable achievement in the magazines. The exception is the Gregory Trust, which restricts itself to young poets under 30 and although concerned with ability demands slightly less visible success. Bursary conditions vary considerably from region to region. Check directly with your RAAs — see Appendix 2 for full details.

The best sources for information on competitions are library notice boards, classified adverts in places like *Time Out* and the little magazines, in particular both *Orbis* (199 The Long Shoot, Nuneaton, Warwickshire CV11 6JQ) and *Quartos* (see Appendix 2). Some details are included in *The Writers' and Artists' Yearbook* and *The Writer's Handbook* and in lists produced by both The Poetry Society and The Poetry Library, while the fullest list of both competitions and awards is the Book Trust's *Guide to Literary Prizes, Grants and Awards*. See appendix 2 details of these organisations.

18
Readings and Workshops

You go into a room full of chairs and sit down. People are hushed. At the far end someone approaches a lectern and places papers on it. They read. The audience listens, coughs. When the voice stops, there is applause. No one shouts. There are no encores.

Poetry readings have long been a subject for debate. Should poetry be read out loud? Is there any purpose in it? Any entertainment? Any value? Poet and critic Antony Conran claims that spoken poetry is "to drama as chamber music is to symphony. Ideally it should happen in one's living-room, late at night, among friends". Many practitioners regard readings as a sideline to their main activity of writing for the page. Some go as far as to dismiss public presentations altogether. Anglo-Welsh poet Raymond Garlick insists: "Poetry is not a performing act and the absolute poem is the written one." Yet the majority see readings as legitimate. Bob Cobbing, Adrian Mitchell, Ivor Cutler and others actually claim performance as poetry's prime purpose. Benjamin Zephania, Linton Kwesi Johnson and Attila the Stockbroker make it their *raison d'etre*. That of course is how it began. Ezra Pound (in *Poetry* 1916): "Therefore we read again for the one-thousand-one-hundred-and-eleventh time that poetry is made to entertain. As follows: 'The beginnings of English poetry . . . made by a rude warfaring people for the entertainment of men-at-arms . . ., " — who certainly couldn't *read* and would have had their poetry chanted at them, recited, *sung*.

It is this element of entertainment which causes dissension. Some serious poets do not wish themselves mistaken for stand-up comics. Gesticulations, eccentric delivery and a line in instant imagery do not, they argue, elevate the art. "Readings may be good for trade," as C.H. Sisson suggests, but on the whole poetry should be a difficult practice where the reader has to do some of the work. "Form is an extension of content," Olson points out. If it is to be read out loud it has to be composed that way. There are poets whose inept delivery ruins what they've written, and others who can elevate the banal simply by the way they speak.

None the less public readings are a vital component of any poetry scene. Here new works are first heard; it is, after all, a way of giving them publication. The poets read not only for the audiences but for themselves. "If ever I'm in doubt or want to perfect something, I read it aloud" — Alan Sillitoe. It is always important to see how a new work sounds. You can try this yourself — in the bathroom, alone if you want — just listen to the poem stretched out across the length of time it actually takes to speak it. You'll hear all the bumps and be made aware of its failures. Adrian Mitchell said once that when a poem had a mistake in it perhaps the voice would slide over it the first time and make it sound all right but by the second reading it would catch and rub and in the end it would have to be changed. He couldn't keep using it in a reading knowing it to be wrong.

Poetry readings can be difficult if you're not used to listening to concentrated speech and particularly if they happen to be presented badly or if the poets read for too long. Yet often they are the places where poetry becomes "activated" and can reach an audience for the first time. Here's American Jack Anderson on "Reading Poems Aloud":

> People interested in poetry usually tend to be interested in poets, too. Though critical purists may insist — and rightly — that a poem should exist as an autonomous object, it is hard to suppress curiosity about the person who made the poem: what does he look like? What does he sound like? No wonder poetry readings are popular.
>
> The sheer fascination of associating poem and person often prevents even dull readings from being total disasters. Yet some readings are clearly better than others. As poet and reader, and a listener to fellow poets, I find that the occasions I most enjoy are those which are quite frankly treated as performances.
>
> That word "performance" is anathema to many poets, who regard it as synonymous with "falsity" or "insincerity". It need not be. To recognize a poetry reading as a performance is simply to recognize the necessity of presenting one's self and one's poems in the best possible light.
>
> But I want to do this honestly. I do not want to deceive anyone. And as a member of the audience for other poets, I do not want to be deceived. Thus I deplore a platform manner so outrageous that it distracts from the actual poetry. Conversely, there is no reason why a poet should minimize himself or his work. I have encountered a few poets — including very good ones — who are dreadfully incompetent readers. They mumble, they drone, they mutter and sputter and, finally, they massacre their poems in public. These occasions are embarrassing. One accomplishes nothing by making one's poems sound dull.
>
> So much about poetry involves solitude. One writes alone, and even when a poem is published a poet may not know how it affects anyone else. A poetry reading allows a writer to share his work directly with others. I like reading my poems aloud. I hope my audiences also like hearing them.

Poets on Stage: The Some Symposium

If there are no readings in your area — and you can find out through the local library or your Regional Arts Association — try listening to recordings of Dylan Thomas, the archetypical declaimer who affected a whole generation, to Michael Horovitz's *Poetry Olympics*, to ranters like Lemn Sissay, Joolz and John Cooper Clark or to Ernst Jandl, Bob Cobbing, and the sound poets to hear just what can be done. Betty Mulcahy's *How To Speak A Poem* (Autolycus Press) offers good advice on the formal approach. Joining a writers' group ought to be your next step. There are three main types:

1. *Writers' circles and local literary societies* — usually long-established and often formal. They place great emphasis on publication and the prestige it can bring. Their prime concerns are fiction writing (particularly for women's magazines), the novel, articles and fillers. Financial reward is important. As a consequence poetry — which a good many members actually practice — takes second place.

2. *Creative-writing classes* — run by the extra-mural departments of colleges, local education authorities and in some cases sponsored by Regional Arts Associations. Poetry is well up on their curriculum, perhaps because so many students demand that it be so. Classes are normally in the charge of someone with a literary reputation whose job it is to cover the whole range of writing styles and kinds. Guest speakers are invited and often these are poets able to give first hand practical advice. A feature of creative-writing classes are their criticism sessions run by the tutor individually or often more beneficially as a group activity in class. This public dissection of your efforts is vital if you are to learn and improve. If you seek publication you cannot avoid criticism. Classes toughen you up. Many also run a magazine or anthology, appointing an editor from among their students and using school or college equipment to do the printing. Charges — even the recently inflated evening-class enrolment costs — still represent excellent value.

3. *Writers' groups* are a general category covering all the rest. These range from science-fiction writers convening in the local library once a month to poets meeting weekly in a pub. They include variants such as *worker writer groups*, which have community bias and non-academic approach, and *creative-writing groups for the unemployed* which run during daytime, often with government help. The trend, if there is one, is towards performance. Poets have always been

concerned with the public presentation of their work but lately fiction writers have shown an interest as well.

These groups — of whatever sort and whatever standard — are an important experience and provide a real benefit to the newcomer. They are places where you can meet others like yourself, exchange ideas, solve problems, remove difficulties. You will learn to improve, give and obtain criticism, and most importantly cease operating in a vacuum. Contact helps, and if you are touchy a writers' group will soon smooth you out.

In recent times there has been a vogue for club and pub poetry cabarets which cater for poetry as a performance art. No gentle recitations here — this is the arena of histrionics, avant-garde posturing and instant entertainment. Much is superficial but it can be fun. On these platforms boundaries have come down. In London check the pages of *Time Out* and *City Limits* or contact *Apples & Snakes* (see Appendix 2). Elsewhere check the public noticeboards and keep your ear to the ground.

The more traditional writers' groups are easier to track down. Begin by asking at your local library to see if there is a group meeting in your district, or write to your Regional Arts Association. If there are none could you consider starting one yourself? All you need is use of a room in a pub, library or school and a few letters to local newspapers inviting those of a like mind to meet you there. It doesn't matter at all in the beginning if no one in the group has any standing or specific literary achievement. Simply the act of reading your work and talking about it will be of help.

If you experience difficulty obtaining information, consult Jill Dick's *Writers' Circles*, a 32-page compilation of some 400 addresses countrywide. This is obtainable from Laurence Pollinger Ltd, 18 Maddox Street, London, W1R OEU. The Federation of Worker Writers and Community Publishers (see Appendix 2) also produces a list of the many groups affiliated to their association. If you live in or around London check with the *Poetry Society* or the *Poetry Library* (see Appendix 2).

19
How To Get Better

You will never arrive if you're any good. The struggle's the thing.
Ivor Cutler

But you can improve. If the poems keep coming back and the writing class is a disaster what can you do? The simple, obvious thing. Read. Make sure you know what's going on in contemporary literature. Read the novels but mostly read the poems. Read widely, don't let there be any areas of writing about which you are unaware.

No one can write the same after *Ulysses*. *Ulysses* changed everything. But people do write as though *Ulysses* never happened, let alone Beckett. These people simply imitate the act of being a writer, a deliberately anachronistic act, like writing a five-act verse drama in Shakespearean English.

B.S. Johnson in *The Imagination on Trial*

It happens too often. Poets just don't appreciate what is going on around them. They churn out their stuff with no consideration for the context in which they work. It's creation with scant knowledge, like building skyscrapers knowing nothing about glass. I've even heard some novice poets seriously claim that they do not wish to read the poetry of others because the ideas there may contaminate their own. The reverse should be the case. Be contaminated. Plagiarize. Borrow. Write in the style of anyone you admire. Re-work. There is nothing new in this, it's been going on since before Shakespeare. No one can ultimately write in isolation. No one can operate entirely without influence. Old ideas recycle, you come upon them time and again.

I'm not suggesting here that you should simply steal other people's work when you can't manage your own. But there is nothing wrong with an idea or a story rewritten or a style or stance reused. Yet do as Pound insisted: *Make it new*.

Read as much contemporary poetry as you can. Begin with anthologies: Blake Morrison and Andrew Motion's *Penguin Book of Contemporary British Poetry*, Dannie Abse's *Hutchinson Book of Post-war British Poems*, Edward Lucie-Smith's *British Poetry Since 1945* (Penguin), Seamus Heaney and Ted Hughes' *The Rattle Bag* (Faber), Andrew Crozier and Tim Longville's *A Various Art* (Paladin), the highly electic *The New British Poetry* (Paladin), *Vital Signs* — Ronald Wallace's selection of contemporary American poetry from the university presses (Wisconsin), Geoffrey Moore's *Penguin Book Of American Verse*, Helen Vendler's *The Faber Book Of Contemporary American Poetry*, plus Donald Allen and George F. Buttrick's *The Postmoderns; The New American Poetry Revised* (Grove) and *In The American Tree*, a language poetry anthology edited by Ron Silliman (NPF). These last two might be harder to get hold of than the others but persistence will pay. Try the bookshops listed in Appendix 1. Read the poet's own books, read the little mags and the small presses. Don't get stuck with one style or in one area. Be eclectic. Read poetry translated. "English literature has made us ignorant of what is going on in the world" — Peter Redgrove. Read the great modernists — Pound, Eliot — and read the great poets of the past. If you find it difficult, persevere. Don't expect all poetry to be the same. Philip Ward, owner of Oleander Press and a poet himself, has mapped out 500 great books to be enjoyed over 50 years in his guide *A Lifetime's Reading*. Here you would encounter Eliot in year 32, Yeats in 39 and unaccountably have to await until year 44 before you get to Ezra Pound. That might be too long but at least it is a plan. Look up the recommendations of others and follow them. You can't read everything. Use all the maps you find.

Almost as important as reading is allowing yourself time.

> What is needed for good poems, besides exceptional talent, is patience, and a willingness to live, if necessary, in some solitude and obscurity while one's life and talent mature, even if that takes many years. People instinctively wise know this and do not attempt to force their work into the open before it is ripe.
>
> John Haines, *Living Off The Country*

But if you wait for inspiration to strike, like one of those rays of light striking through cloud in a Blake engraving, then you won't write very much. You must keep at it, regularly, persistently. Set yourself time, insulate yourself, work. Throw out the rubbish as you create it, and as you proceed you'll improve.

> I find the more I write the more I enjoy writing and the better I write.
> Michael Moorcock

If you don't keep and mature your force and above all have time and quiet to perfect your work, you will be writing things not much better than you did five years ago . . . otherwise, what might be strength is only crudeness and what might be insight is only observation. You will write about life, but never life itself.

Sarah Orne Jewett

There are some times, however, when no matter how long you sit in front of your typewriter or notepad nothing will come. Even if you've allowed yourself time and kept yourself from phone, family and visitors you may still be unable to do anything more than look through the window. "If you're bored, stop," says James Simmons. But this isn't just boredom, this is blockage. The poet Ken Smith solves it best:

> Sometimes I think it's gone forever. Over the years I've learned not to sweat it. To relax and let it go or come as it will, and conclude that my purpose in life is not to write poetry but to live my life. Therefore I do that, setting snares to trap the poem where there seems to be one in the air. There are times when, having finished a run of work, I know I'm empty — or that vein is worked out and there's no point repeating what I've already done. Therefore I mooch about, hoping to surprise myself: mucking about in a library with no particular book in mind, letting myself find something I know nothing about; going on a journey; finding silence; entering places where English is not spoken; sleeping a lot and dreaming; encountering strangers; recording strange events, consulting oracles, collecting images, getting drunk, staying sober, attempting to cleanse the doors of perception or forget what I know. And absolute patience till the poem begins to nudge.

Read what you've written. Revise. Few poems are finished just as they come. Most require work and then more work. Give up unless you are really obsessed. There are too many poets. But you should know that by now.

Join a workshop, listen to what poetry programmes there are on radio, borrow tapes, and keep reading. Read the poetry reviews in the Sunday papers and the small-press listings in the little magazines.

Don't imagine it's just you that has this mantle of genius thrust upon you; this ability to create poetry is no mystic, intangible thing. If you don't know just what you are doing, don't imagine anyone else will.

> Great poetry may contain great wisdom, but that is never the reason it is great poetry. It is not enough. It is the form, the shaping of the language which makes poetry endure. It is not what it meant to the poet that is important, rather it is the effect . . .

Judson Jerome

Poetry first is work, concentration, practice. And then something else, undefinable. You try, but as Cecil Harnby complained to Ted Wilentz of Corinth Books:

Here you are at 40, a poet. If you're famous you wonder if it's temporary and whether your poetry is really any good or not. If you're not famous, you wonder what you've been devoting your life to. If you're good, you'll never really know it.

Appendix 1: Bookshops

As most bookshops sell poetry, why is there a need for specialists? The average shop will stock a little contemporary poetry, it is true — perhaps the better-selling Penguin anthologies, a selection of Hughes and Heaney from Faber, Philip Larkin, Roger McGough, a few Oxford anthologies, a dash of Bloodaxe, maybe a volume or two from the local poet if they've been pushy enough. Beyond that — a jumble of Betjeman and Fiona Pitt-Kethley. Very little else. Range is the answer. The average shop stocks only from a narrow selection of proven sellers. The large bookshops in the bigger towns do better. But if you want American poetry, new British or Irish material or particularly the small-press publications and little magazines, then you'll have to hunt.

Many shops will allow you to order any standard British book of poetry in print. If they operate this service efficiently, provide you with catalogues and make no special-order surcharges then take advantage of it. A number of local shops — particularly those in university towns — can be important sources of supply. But for the full selection — small presses especially — you'll be obliged to go elsewhere.

The following bookshops are all poetry specialists of one sort or another. Many issue catalogues. If you live near them try a visit. All are willing to handle orders by post and will deal with your enquiries even if these are of a general nature. "Please supply me with a selection of recent poetry magazines," for example. When writing remember to enclose a s.a.e.

London Area

Collected Works, (small press & second-hand), 3 Melbourne Terrace, Melbourne Grove, London SE22 8RE (081 299 4195)

Compendium Bookshop, (new, contemporary, small press, imports), 234 Camden High Street, London NW1 (071 267 1525)

Dillons University Bookshop, (new, contemporary, second-hand, imports), 82 Gower Street, London WC1 (071 636 1577)

Four Provinces Bookshop (Irish), 244 Grays Inn Road, London WC1X 8JR (071 833 3022)

W & A Foyle (new, contemporary, imports), 119 Charing Cross Road, London WC2 (071 437 5660)

Green Ink Bookshop (Irish), 8 Archway Mall, London N19 (071 263 4748)

Owl Bookshop (new, contemporary), 211 Kentish Town Road, London NW5 (071 485 7793)

Iain Sinclair Books, (British, American and European poetry, new & second-hand), 28 Albion Drive, London E8 4ET (081 254 8571)

Bernard Stone, The Turret Bookshop (new, contemporary, imports, small press), 42 Lamb's Conduit Street, London WC1 (071 405 6058)

Waterstone's (new, contemporary), 193 Kensington High Street, London W8. (071 937 8432)

Waterstone's (new, contemporary), Hampstead High Street, London NW3 (071.794.1098)

Outside London

Blackwells (new & second-hand, imports, contemporary), Broad Street, Oxford OX1 3BQ (0865 792792)

The Book Shop (new, contemporary), 20 High Street, Princes Risborough, Bucks HP17 OAX

N.F.Brookes (second-hand, imports, Polish), 12a Queens Rd, Brighton, BN1 3WA (0273 23105)

First Of May, 43, Candlemakers Row, Edinburgh EH1 2QB

Paul Green (small press, imports), 83b London Road, Peterborough, Cambs.

Gateway Paperbacks (new, contemporary), Chester Street, Shrewsbury SY1 1NB (0743 55109)

Hatchards (new, contemporary), 2 Brook Street, Kingston-on-Thames, Surrey KT1 2HA)

Hazeldene Bookshop (new, contemporary, small press), 61 Renshaw Street, Liverpool L1 2SJ (051 708 8780)

The Independent Bookshop (new, contemporary, African and US imports), 69 Surrey St, Sheffield S1 2LH

LAMP Community Bookshop, (new, contemporary, small press & community publishing), 22 Church Street, Leigh, Lancs (0942 606667)

Mushroom Bookshop (contemporary, new, imports) 10 Heathcote St, Nottingham NG1 3AA (0602 582506)

Oriel Bookshop, (new, contemporary, small press, imports, Welsh & Anglo-Welsh), The Friary, Cardiff CF1 4AA (0222 395548)

The Poetry Bookshop*, (new & second-hand, contemporary, imports, large small press stock), 22 Broad Street, Hay-on-Wye, Hereford HR3 5DB (0497 820 305)

The Poetry Business (new, contemporary, small press), 51 Byram Arcade, Westgate, Huddersfield HD11 1ND (0484 434840)

Public House Bookshop, (new, contemporary, imports, small presses), 21 Little Preston Street, Brighton (0233 28257)

Peter Riley, Books (out of print items, second-hand, small presses), 27 Sturton Street, Cambridge CB1 2QU

Third Eye Bookshop (Scottish), 350 Sauchiehall Street, Glasgow G2 3JD (041 332 7521)

The University Bookshop (new, contemporary, imports), 91 University Road, Belfast BT7 1NL (0232 666302)

The Wall Bookshop (new, contemporary), The Arts Centre, St Mary-at-the-Wall, Church Street, Colchester (0206 577301)

This list is by no means definitive. Regular updatings are produced by both The Poetry Library and the ALP (see Appendix 2).

Appendix 2: Organizations of Interest to Poets

Apples & Snakes. Organised by Ruth Harrison and Paul Beasley from Room 2, Peter Pan Block, 23 Ladywell Lodge, Slagrove Place, London SE13 7HT (tel:081 690 9368). Britain's principal performance poetry agency and event promoter. It mounts a regular weekly poetry cabaret in central London, organises national poetry tours, publishes anthologies of performance poets and helps organisers anywhere who show an interest in booking stand-up poets with something to say. Auditions to join Apple & Snakes' roster can be made either in person — you are expected to do 15 minutes in their offices — or by sending in an audition tape.

Arts Councils and Regional Arts Association. The Arts Council of Great Britain and its devolved committees, the Scottish, Northern Irish and Welsh Arts Council, have a responsibility "to develop and improve knowledge, understanding and practice of the arts, and to increase their accessibility to the public". As far as literature is concerned, this means subsidy to national bodies such as the Poetry Society and provision of grant aid to mainstream poetry publishers and literary magazines. Provision in Scotland, Northern Ireland and Wales has traditionally been much better than in England.

The principal service the Arts Council of Great Britain makes for literature, however, is the allocation of financial aid to the regions via the Arts Association. These bodies, which also raise additional funds from local government, industry, charitable trusts and private individuals, have a responsibility for the arts at a local level. Service varies from region to region and much depends on the individual initiative. Activities of interest to poets can include the following:

— The publishing of a regional literary magazine
— Organisation of and support for poetry readings.
— Small-scale, usually short-term, writers' bursaries. These have included some quite exciting residencies at libraries, local radio stations, prisons, hospitals, colleges and other institutions, where poets have been on call providing readings, talks and surgeries.
— Poetry competitions
— Literary festivals
— Subsidies to small presses and local poetry magazines.
— Subsidies to writers' workshops and similar groups.
— Critical services for poetry along the lines of the scheme pioneered by the Poetry Society.
— The publishing of directories of local writers, workshops, groups, guidelines for poets seeking publication, lists of markets, advice to reading organisers etc.

All arts associations provide advice and assistance and try to encourage poets – both the novice and the experienced.

Regional Arts Associations

Buckinghamshire Arts Association, Arts Officer: Pat Swell, 55 High Street, Aylesbury, Bucks HP20 1SA (tel: 0296 434704)

East Midlands Arts Association, Literature Officer: Debbie Hicks, Mountfields House, Forest Rd, Loughborough, Leicestershire, LE11 3HU (tel: 0509 218292)

Eastern Arts, Literature Officer: Richard Ings, Cherry Hinton Hall, Cherry Hinton Road, Cambridge, CB1 4DW. (tel: 0223 215355)

Greater London Arts, Director: Trevor Vibert, 20 Gainsford Street, London SE1 2NE. (tel: 071 403 9013)

Lincolnshire & Humberside Arts, Principal Officer, Media: David Baker, St Hugh's, Newport, Lincoln, LN1 3DN. (tel: 0522 533555)

Merseyside Arts, Drama/Literature Officer: Theresa Griffin, Graphic House, Duke St, Liverpool L1 4JE. (tel: 051 709 0671)

North Wales Arts Association, Literature Officer: John Clifford Jones, 10 Wellfield House, Bangor, Gwynedd, LL57 1ER. (tel: 0248 353248)

North West Arts, Literature Officer: Christine Bridgwood, 12 Harter St, Manchester, M1 6YH(tel: 061 228 3062)

Northern Arts, Literature Officer: Don Watson, 9-10 Osborne Tce, Jesmond, Newcastle-upon-Tyne, NE2 1NZ. (tel: 091 281 6334)

South East Arts, Literature Officer: Charmian Stowell, 10 Mount Ephraim, Tunbridge Wells, Kent, TN4 8AS (tel: 0892 515210)

South East Wales Arts, Literature Officer: R.T.Mole, Victoria St, Cwmbran, Gwent, NP44 3YT (tel: 0633 875075)

South West Arts, Literature Officer: Ingrid Squirrell, Bradninch Place, Gandy St, Exeter, EX4 3LS (tel: 0392 218188)

Southern Arts, Literature Officer: Jane Spiers, 19 Southgate St, Winchester, Hampshire, SO23 9DQ (tel: 0962 55099)

West Midlands Arts, Literature Officer: David Hart, 82 Granville St, Birmingham, B1 2LH. (tel: 021 631 3121)

West Wales Association For The Arts, Literature Officer: Liza Prickett, Red Street, Carmarthen, Dyfed, SA31 1QL (tel: 0267 234248)

Yorkshire Arts Association, Literature Officer: Jennifer Barraclough, Glyde House, Little Horton Lane, Bradford, West Yorks, BD5 OBQ (tel: 0274 723051)

There are no arts associations in Scotland.

Arts Councils

Arts Council (Eire), 70 Merrion Square, Dublin 2. (tel: Dublin 611840)

Arts Council Of Great Britain, Literature Director: Alastair Niven, 14 Great Peter Street, London, SW1P 3NQ. (tel: 071 333 0100)

Arts Council Of Northern Ireland, Literature Director: Michael Longley, 181a Stranmillis Rd, Belfast 9. (tel: 0232 381 591)

Scottish Arts Council, Literature Director: Walter Cairns, 12 Manor Place, Edinburgh, EH3 7DD (tel: 031 226 6051)

Welsh Arts Council, Museum Place, Cardiff, CF1 3NX. (tel: 0222 394711).

The Arvon Foundation, founded by Ted Hughes, John Moat and John Fairfax, runs residential courses for people of all ages over sixteen where a chance is given to meet and work with practising writers. There are two centres − both rural: Totleigh Barton, a thatched manor house dating from the eleventh century, near Okehampton, and Lumb Bank, a large eighteenth-century mill-owner's house set in twenty acres of pastureland in the Pennines. Courses usually run for five days and are in the charge of two tutors − both writers with an established reputation − and often include a guest reader. There is a strong emphasis on poetry. The Arvon Foundation receives financial aid from the Arts Associations and although able to subsidize course places to some degree is still obliged to charge. Current rates are in the region of £155 a week. The Arvon Poetry Competition, run at three year intervals, is the biggest of its kind with a first prize of £5000. Further details can be obtained from the Foundation either at Totleigh Barton, Sheepwash, Devon EX21 5NS, or at Lumb Bank, Heptonstall, Hebden Bridge, West Yorkshire HX7 6DF

The Association of Little Presses was formed in 1966 as a "loosely knit association of individuals running little presses who have grouped together for mutual self-help". It acted at first as a pressure group to extend the availability of grant aid and later as an information exchange, advice centre and general promoter of the benefits of small publishing. ALP has a strong bias towards poetry and creative writing and currently represents over 300 publishers and associates throughout Britain and Ireland. Membership costs £10 and is open to both presses and interested individuals. The Association produces a *Catalogue Of Small Press Books In Print*; a twice-yearly magazine *PALPI* (Poetry And Little Press Information) which gives details of recent small-press and other poetry publications; an *ALP Newsletter* of printing and distribution tips, *Getting Your Poetry Published*, a pamphlet of basic advice and the precursor to this book; and an introductory guide *Publish It Yourself — Not Too Difficult After All*. ALP organises bookfairs, exhibitions and gatherings around the country an offers and unrivalled service, by post (with sae) and by telephone, giving information on how you can publish yourself and what you can do with it when you have. ALP Co-ordinator is Bob Cobbing, 89a Petherton Road, London N5 2QT. (tel: 071 226 2657); Chairman is Bill Griffiths (tel: 091 581 6738).

Book Trust (formerly The National Book League) at Book House, 45 East Hill, London SW18 2QZ (tel: 081 870 9055) is an independent educational charity promoting books and reading. It provides a book information service, administers a number of literary prizes and publishes a wide range of books, pamphlets and guides for readers. Of particular interest to poets are the *Guide to Literary Prizes, Grants and Awards* and the quarterly magazine *Book News*. The exhibitions department organises touring exhibitions of book collections including a number based around poetry.

European Association For The Promotion Of Poetry at Blijde Inkomststraat 9, B-3000 Leuven, Belgium is the home of the European Poetry Library and Centre for Research, Translation and Documentation. Centre of the euroverse for EC members. The Association is based around the annual Poetry Festival in Leuven from where it administers the European Prize for translation of poetry, publishes bi-lingual volumes by European poets and a poetry magazine *Pi*. The Association works in four languages: Dutch, French, English and German. Membership costs 1000 BF.

Federation Of Worker Writers And Community Publishers was formed in 1976 to promote working class writing. It has almost forty member groups around the country including both writing workshops and community publishers. All groups are committed to writing based on working class experience with a particular welcome for the work of women, black and gay writers. The majority of members have a strong poetry interest and include Centreprise, Liverpool 8 Writers and Bristol Broadsides. The Federation runs an education day, conferences and poetry competitions. It produces anthologies of working class writing, a catalogue of member group publications, a series of leaflets on self-publishing and a newsletter, *Fed News*. For information contact Pat Smart, 232 Boodecroft, Stockbridge Village, Liverpool L28 4EL.

The Little Magazine Collection and **The Poetry Store** are held at the University College London Library and are the fruits of Geoffrey Soar and David Miller's long standing interest in UK alternative publishing with its almost overwhelming obsession with poetry. Begun in 1964 the Little Magazines Collection now runs to more than 3000 titles of mainly underground/alternative/radical literary productions such as *Tlaloc*, *Poetmeat* and *Second Aeon*. The Poetry Store has at least 6000 items with a fair stress on experimental work. Anyone who is interested can consult the collection although it does help to have some idea of what you would like to see. Bring evidence of identity for a smooth ride. The collections can be accessed by visiting the Manuscripts and Rare Books Room at the University in Gower Street, London WC1E 6BT between 10.00am and 5.00pm on weekdays. Tel: 071 387 7050 ext. 2617.

Municipal Libraries are an underrated source of information. Join if you haven't, borrow their poetry, request the stuff that's missing, check the notice boards. Most local librarians will be well informed on where writers' groups meet, who the local poets are and what publishing goes on. Increasingly libraries themselves are used as bases for writing classes and poetry events. Use the service; it's still free.

National Convention Of Poets And Small Presses. A lively and highly accessible amateur jamboree of writers and poetry publishers held at a different and usually provincial venue each year. Based around a small press bookfair and exhibition the weekend event is dominated by marathon poetry readings which to get the best out of require stamina on the part of participants and audience alike. There is no central organizing committee – bids to host future conventions being made in person at the event itself. So far it has visited Liverpool, Hastings, Corby, Dartford, Stamford, Norwich and North Shields. Check with the Poetry Library or the Poetry Society to find out where it is this year.

Northern Arts Poetry Library is situated at the County Library, The Willows, Morpeth, Northumberland NE6 1TA and has over 6000 volumes including virtually all mainstream poetry published in UK since 1968. Membership is free and open to residents of the North East and Cumbria. Loans may be made by post.

Oriel Bookshop, now situated in new premises at The Friary, Cardiff CF1 4AA, specialises in twentieth century poetry, has a strong interest in small press activity, operates a mail order service, runs a critical service for writers, hosts poetry readings, publishes at regular intervals *Small Presses In The UK and Ireland An Address List* and provides information on poetry competitions, local workshops, groups and other poetry activities. Its collection of Welsh and Anglo-Welsh poetry is unrivalled anywhere in the world. Oriel is owned and operated by the Welsh Arts Council. Tel: (0222 395548)

Password is an Arts Council funded agency representing a number of small poetry publishers. It runs courses suitable for poets interested in self-publishing, offers consultancy advice and publishes a catalogue of its participants' publications. 23 New Mount Street, Manchester M4 4DE (tel: 061 953 4009)

PLR is the long-fought-for Public Lending Right which allows authors of books borrowed free from public libraries to gain some financial recompense. The scheme works through an analysis of loans from selected sample libraries across the country multiplied to arrive at a national average. A loan earns approximately 1.39p. Not one poet appeared in the recently compiled top 100 most borrowed authors although down among the lesser fish there is always a chance. Authors need to register their titles in order to benefit.

Full details from PLR Registrar, Bayheath House, Prince Regent Street, Stockton-on-Tees, Cleveland TS18 1DF (tel: 0642 604699)

The Poetry Association of Scotland, founded by John Masefield in 1924, was formerly known as the Scottish Association for the Speaking of Verse. Secretary is Robin Bell. It promotes poetry through readings and related activities from its headquarters at 38 Dovecot Road, Edinburgh EH12 7LE.

The Poetry Book Society was founded in 1953 by T.S. Eliot to foster the love of poetry by providing the uninitiated with an approved selection from the best newly published books of the day. Today and for an annual fee of £19.50 the Society's 2000 members receive a quarterly new book of verse, an annual anthology and the PBS Quarterly Bulletin. Members are also able to purchase from a vast selection of PBS 'recommendations' at reduced prices. For those not near a bookshop it is an excellent way of building a mainstream poetry library. For the really keen the Society also offers membership 'B', bringing you 21 new books annually for £99.50. Contact the Membership Department, PBS, 21 Earl's Court Square, London SW5 9DE (tel: 071 244 9792).

The Poetry Business is a resource centre run by Peter Sansom and associates from Floor 4, Byram Arcade, Westgate, Huddersfield HD1 1ND (tel: 0484 434840). Based around a small bookshop and poetry library the Business provides a critical reading service which offers participants guidance on where they might publish their work, an annual pamphlet competition, monthly workshop writing days together with hands on advice on poetry as a whole. The Business's publishing arm includes *The North* magazine and the *Smith/Doorstop* series of booklets. Send for their free catalogue.

Poetry Ireland is an all-Ireland poetry organisation supported by arts councils both north and south of the border. Known best for its quality quarterly *Poetry Ireland Review* the organisation also acts as a book club offering members books at concessionary prices, publishes a bi-monthly Newsletter of upcoming events and competitions and organises reading tours for both Irish and foreign poets. Poetry Ireland also administers the Austin Clarke Library of over 6000 volumes. Director is Theo Dorgan; Administrator is Pat Boran. 44 Upper Mount Street, Dublin 2. (tel: 01 610320).

The Poetry Library (formerly The Arts Council Poetry Library) is now situated in the South Bank Centre, London, one of the world's largest arts centres. It is a unique assemblage of modern verse in book, booklet, poster, broadsheet, poemcard, record, tape and video form. It is the best collection on any single site in Britain. Librarian Mary Enright describes the Library as "a unique institution offering free and open access to poetry form all over the world, written or translated into English. All varieties are represented

– children's, concrete, rap, surrealist, verse drama, experimental and traditional.'' The library produces ''awareness'' lists of information on competitions, magazines, bookshops, festivals, workshops and evening classes. It also has a wealth of advice on publishing for the new poet. Information and lists are free on receipt of sae.

In his introduction to the 6th edition of the Library's catalogue Philip Larkin described the venture as ''one of the occasional pure flowerings of imagination for which the English are so seldom given credit: the creation of a public library devoted entirely to modern poetry. Nothing else: no criticism, no biography, simply books by well known poets and unknown poets side by side in the democracy of alphabetical order.''

Membership is free. The Library functions as any other public library with loans, requests, inter-library lending, etc. Its hours are possibly the longest of all libraries – open seven days a week from 11.00 am to 8.00 pm daily. The Poetry Library can be found on Level 5, Royal Festival Hall, South Bank Centre, London SE1 8XX. (Tel 071 921 0943/0664.) Nearest tube/BR: Embankment and Waterloo.

Poetry Listing compiled by David Hart on a trusty Amstrad is an irregular publication which attempts to provide an overview of the whole of published contemporary English Language poetry worldwide. The survey is total, not limiting itself to the recently published and as the only such check-list currently available is indispensable. Don't look here for markets for your verse but use it as a map of available contemporary poetry which gives lots of advice on what to read next. Copies from Wood Wind Publications, 42 All Saints Rd, Kings Heath, Birmingham B14 7LL.

Poetry London Newsletter details all current poetry activity in the capital from listings of readings, workshops and classes to reviews of little presses, major poetry books together with articles on obtaining funding, starting a poetry group and how to run a reading. Write to Leon Cych at 26 Clacton Rd, London E17 8AR.

The Poetry Society is a national organisation dedicated solely to the promotion of poets and poetry. It was founded in 1909 and has been rolling forward ever since, embracing alternatively the radical and conservative elements of British poetry. Its present phase is one of liberal inclusiveness although it still has a substantial number of detractors. It is based at The National Poetry Centre, a converted five-storey Victorian house at 21 Earl's Court Square, London SW5 9DE (tel: 071 373 2551), under its director Chris Green. Membership costs £20 with reductions to £15 and £12 if you live outside London or are a student, OAP or claimant. Society activities include:
– Regular reading and events at the National Poetry Centre.
– An annual National Poetry Competition which awards over £4500 in prizes and is one of the most prestigious in Britain.

- An education department sponsored by W.H.Smiths running a Poets in Schools scheme, writing courses and offering professional advice and information to teachers.
- *The National Poetry Secretariat*, which provides financial assistance to literature festivals and hundreds of readings throughout the UK. Organisers outside London are able to book poets through the NPS (tel: 071 370 6929) and often obtain subsidy towards their fees. Registration of poets at the NPS is free.
- Spoken-verse examinations taken by several thousand candidates starting with children aged six through all stages to the adult gold medal.
- *The Poetry Review*, a quarterly magazine, which has included all the major twentieth-century poets in its much varied seventy-five year run of publication.
- A small poetry bookshop which operates a mail-order service.
- A newsletter and information leaflets on poetry magazines and the perils of publication.
- A number of awards and prizes including the Alice Hunt Bartlett Award, The Dylan Thomas Award and the European Poetry Translation Prize.
- A critical service for the work of members.

The Society is funded by the Arts Council of Great Britain and is run by an elected council of eminent literati under president Dannie Abse.

Quartos magazine – a bi-monthly writers' forum and competition news. Subscription £10.00 from BCM-Writer, London WC1N 3XX. Vaguely amateur as a forum but certainly the best single source of information of poetry competitions and other events anywhere in the UK.

Schools' Poetry Association. Much reduced in influence since its magazine *Schools Poetry Review* was subsumed by Stanley Thornes Ltd into its journal on English and the National Curriculum, *Creative Language*. The Association runs the *Shell Young Poet Of The Year* competition, fields a team of experienced workshop leaders and publishes poetry broadsheets. Membership is informal although full benefits come only to subscribers at £26.55 of *Creative Language*. Details from David Orme, 27 Pennington Close, Colden Common, Nr Winchester, Hants S21 1UR.

Scottish Poetry Library holds a comprehensive collection of poetry written in Scotland embellished with work from elsewhere in the world. In order to reach parts of Scotland that other organisations do not the Library tours with *Poetry Travels*, a converted Post Office van. Loans are free from the premises, those by post subject to a small charge. The Library publishes a newsletter, a catalogue together with lists of Scottish magazines and poetry publishers. Memberships costs £7.50. Director is Tess Ransford, Librarian is Tom Hubbard. Tweedale Court, 14 High Street, Edinburgh EH1 1TE. (tel: 031 557 2876)

Small Press Group of Britain was founded in 1988 by John Nicholson and others in order to increase public awareness of the valuable role of small presses throughout the UK. This is done by running national and international bookfairs on some scale, publishing a monthly newsletter *Small Press Monthly*, acting as an information exchange, publishing the annual *Small Press Yearbook* which lists members' output together with a mine of information on small press publishing and distribution. The SPG's involvement with poetry is by no means central but the Group should be of considerable interest to poets considering self-publishing who wish a more aggressive or commercial approach to their marketing. Membership costs £12.00. Write to the Membership Secretary at BM Bozo, London WC1N 3XX. (tel: 0234 211606)

The Society of Authors, 84 Drayton Gardens, London SW10 9SB (tel: 071.373.6642) and the **Writers' Guild of Great Britain,** 430 Edware Road, London W2 1EH (tel: 071 723 8074), are the two principal writers' trade unions. Although their origins differ, the Writers' Guild originally representing the interests of theatre, film and television writers, both organisations now concern themselves with the whole spectrum of authorship, including poetry. They provide a professional service – principally the supplying of information and advice on the practise of writing and the representing of members' interests to employers, usually publishers, much in the way other trade unions do. The Society of Authors is independent, while the Writers' Guild is affiliated to the TUC. The benefits of membership are commensurate with the status these organisations have within the publishing world. For the part-time writer fees are not cheap – £32 for writers under 35 and £50 otherwise in the case of the Society and 1 per cent of earnings with a bottom fee of £50 in respect of full membership for the Guild. Only professional *published* writers are eligible to join.

The direct benefits to poets would appear to be peripheral but if you've read Chapter 11 on *Cash* you will appreciate that all poets need to work in some allied field as well as verse in order to survive. If that is to be writing of some sort, then membership of the Society or the Guild should be investigated. Both organisations publish a magazine: *The Author* from the Society and *The Writers' Newsletter* from the Guild. Sample copies and information on membership are available on request.

Taliesin Trust is a Welsh version of the Arvon Foundation's residential writing centres situated at Ty Newydd, Llanystumdwy, Cricieth, Gwynedd LL52 OLW (tel: 0766 522811). This seventeenth century house was the last home of Lloyd George. Courses have a poetry element and a bias towards Welsh and Anglo-Welsh interests. Weekly fees begin at £155. Centre directors are Sally Baker Jones and Elis Gwyn Jones.

The Welsh Academy, 3rd Floor, Mount Stuart House, Mount Stuart Square,

Docks, Cardiff CF1 6DQ, (tel: 0222 492025) exists to promote writers and writing in Wales, in the English language. Full membership is by invitation although associate membership at £6 annually is open to all. The Academy organises courses for poets, and promotes readings and conferences. Since 1986 it has been responsible for putting on the annual Cardiff Literature Festival. The Academy organises a number of poetry competitions including the City of Cardiff International which has £3000 in prizes and is open to entrants worldwide. The Academy publishes a newsletter of literary information *BWA*. President is Roland Mathias, Chairman is Gillian Clarke and Secretary is Kevin Thomas.

Welsh Union Of Writers was founded in 1982 with the intention of representing the interests of Welsh writers, much like the Society of Authors and the Writers' Guild. Given the smaller compass within Wales and the higher proportion of working poets the WUW is of considerable interest to Welsh based writers of verse. The Union's magazine *The Works* publishes a large number of poems. Membership costs £10 from secretary Ifor Thomas, 11 Wingate Drive, Llanishen, Cardiff CF4 5LR (tel: 0222 757938).

Appendix 3: The Poet's Library

Ten books which should be on all poets' shelves

- *A dictionary. The Concise Oxford* or *The Shorter Oxford* in two-volume form are the best but if you can't afford them try *Chambers* or *Collins* or even one of the smaller, cheaper Oxford dictionaries. Expect to pay in excess of £10. If you see one that's less expensive it will have a lot of words left out.

- *Roget's Thesaurus* — in editions by Penguin, Sphere, Collins or Longman. Next to a full dictionary probably the single most useful book in a poet's armoury. It is here that you find the alternatives to the word you've thought of, the similes, the vocabulary to fill out your ideas.

- *The Writers' Handbook* (Macmillan), *The Writers' and Artists' Yearbook* (A & C Black). Much recommended. New editions of these two similarly priced volumes are published annually. They are the ultimate handbooks for writers, containing addresses of most English language book and periodical publishers here and abroad, plus information on broadcasting, literary agents, copyright, PLR, books and societies for the writer, translation, income tax, libel, publisher's agreements, proof correction symbols, VAT, subsidiary rights and much more. There is little to choose between them — *Yearbook* has more hard, technical information, the *Handbook* offers opinion. Both have a poetry sections but only the *Handbook* goes into detail on small presses and little magazines.

- *The Catalogue of Small Press Books In Print* (Association of Little Presses), *Small Press Yearbook* (Small Press Group). Two similar annual compendiums of small press activity detailing UK output with descriptions of presses and full addresses. The ALP volume binds in sheets produced by the presses themselves. The *Small Press Yearbook* contains a wealth of data on the techniques of small publishing itself. Both are indexed.

- *Small Presses and Little Magazines of the UK and Ireland - An Address List* (Oriel), *British Literary Periodicals - A Selected Bibliography* (The British Council), *Directory of Poetry Publishers* (Dustbooks), *Poet's Market* (Writers Digest). One or more of these four is a definite requirement. More than 1000 addresses in the Oriel list, compact information on UK magazines from The British Council. The Dustbooks and Writers Digest volumes list presses and magazines worldwide under subject, country of origin and again alphabetically. Their range is terrific but the drawback to the UK user is that they are American based.

● *Fowler's Modern English Usage*, revised by Sir Ernest Gowers (OUP, 1968). The best book for writers uncertain about any points in English grammer, the meaning or respectability of a word or even its pronunciation.

● *The Poets' Manual and Rhyming Dictionary* — Frances Stillman (Thames and Hudson). A good reference work if you use rhyme, making it possible, at a glance, to find the less obvious word. The work doubles as a poet's manual to include a complete reference section on prosody, the handling of language in poetry. It covers everything from basic traditional meters through to the newest developments.

● *Into Print* – Susan Quilliam and Ian Grove-Stephensen (BBC Books, 1990). Subtitled "How to Make Desktop Publishing Work For You" this is actually a pretty good introduction to the technicalities of the printing process covering everything from document design to setting the text.

● *How to Publish Yourself* – Peter Finch (Allison and Busby, 1991) A companion volume to the present *How To Publish Your Poetry* and essential reading for those who wish to follow on from the information contained in Chapter 12. The book covers history, how to set yourself up, the printing process, design, how to cut costs, home printing, the new technology, selling, marketing and promotion, what to do when things go wrong and a thousand other things you would certainly never have thought of yourself. If you only consult one book before embarking on publication then this should be it.

● *How To Enjoy Poetry* — Vernon Scanell (Piatkus, 1983). A handbook on the development of poetry in English, dealing in simple terms wiht the craft, technique, history and contemporary manifestation (readings, competitions, pop poetry) of the form. Almost an owner's manual, it also includes a reading list and a fine section on writing verse for yourself.

Appendix 4: Books on Publishing

Charles N. Aronson: *The Writer Publisher* (Charles N. Aronson, 1976).

Clifford Burke: *Printing It* (Wingbow, 1972).

Michael Scott Cain: *Book Marketing: A Guide to Intelligent Distribution* (Dustbooks, 1981).

Michael Scott Cain: *The Co-Op Publishing Handbook* (Dustbooks, 1978).

David Cherry: *Preparing Artwork for Reproduction* (Batsford, 1976).

Lionel S. Darley: *Introduction to Bookbinding* (Faber, 1977).

Peter Finch: *How To Publish Yourself* (Allison and Busby, 1991) Peter Finch: *Publishing Yourself - Not Too Difficult After All* (ALP, 1990).

John Gough: *Into Print* (Batsford, 1979).

Hart's Rules For Compositors And Readers (Oxford University Press, 1983).

L.M. Hasselstrom: *The Book Book: A Publishing Handbook (for Beginners and Others)* (L.J. Press, 1976).

Bill Henderson (ed.): *The Publish it Yourself Handbook -Literary Tradition & How-To* (Pushcart, 1973).

Norman Hidden: *The Poet's Guide No.1 — How to be Your Own Publisher* (Workshop Press, 1979).

John Laing (ed.): *Do-It-Yourself Graphic Design* (Edbury Press, 1984).

Roy Lewis and John Easson: *Home Publishing and Printing* (David and Charles, 1984).

L.W. Mueller: *How to Publish Your Own Book. A Guide for Authors Who Wish to Publish a Book at their Own Expense* (Harlo Press, 1976).

Harry Mulholland: *Guide to Self-Publishing — An A-Z of Getting Yourself into Print* (Mulholland-Wirral, 1984).

The Oxford Dictionary for Writers and Editors (OUP, 1983).

Dan Poynter: *The Self-Publishing Manual* (Para Publishing, 1989).

Susan Quilliam and Ian Grove-Stephensen: *Into Print* (BBC Books, 1990).

Marilyn and Tom Ross: *Marketing Your Book* (Communications Creativity, 1990).

Herbert Simon: *Introduction to Printing. The Craft of Letterpress* (Faber, 1968).

Ian Templeton: *Publish It Yourself And Make It Pay* (Pikers Pad, 1985).

Audrey and Philip Ward: *The Small Publisher* (Oleander Press, 1979).

Celeste West and Valerie Wheat: *The Passionate Perils of Publishing* (Booklegger, 1978).

Hugh Williamson: *Methods of Book Design* (Yale, 1983).

Adrian Wilson: *The Design of Books* (Gibbs M. Smith Inc., 1974).

Kirty Wilson-Davies & others: *Desktop Publishing* (Kogan Page, 1988).

Jon Wynne-Tyson: *Publishing Your Own Book* (Centaur Press, 1989).

Bibliography

Elliott Anderson and Mary Kinzie (eds.): *The Little Magazine in America: A Modern Documentary History* (Pushcart, 1978).

The Arts Council of Great Britain: *The Arts Council Poetry Library Catalogue* (ACGB, 1981).

Denys Val Baker (ed.): *Little Reviews Anthology 1946* (Eyre and Spottiswoode, 1946).

Michael Baldwin: *The Way To Write Poetry* (Elm Tree Books, 1982).

BBC: *Writing For The BBC* (BBC Publications, 1988).

Julian Birkett: *Word Power — A Guide to Creative Writing* (A. & C. Black, 1983).

Book Trust: *Guide To Literary Prizes, Grants and Awards* (Book Trust, 1989).

John Brady and Jean M. Fredette (eds.): *Fiction Writer's Market* (Writer's Digest, annual).

Judith Butcher: *Typescripts, Proofs and Indexes* (Cambridge University Press, 1980).

Alan Burns and Charles Sugnet (eds.): *The Imagination On Trial* (Allison and Busby, 1981).

Cassell and the Publisher's Association Directory of Publishing (Cassell, annual).

James Charlton (ed.): *The Writer's Quotation Book — A Literary Companion* (Penguin, 1981).

Bob Cobbing: *The Small Press Survey 1990* (ALP, 1990).

Bob Cobbing and Peter Mayer: *Concerning Concrete Poetry* Writers Forum, 1978).

W.A. Copinger and Skone Jones: *Copyright* (Sweet & Maxwell, 1989).

J.A. Cuddon: *A Dictionary of Literary Terms* (Penguin, 1982).

Jill Dick: *Writers' Circles* (Laurence Pollinger Ltd, 1988).

Dianne Doubtfire: *Teach Yourself Creative Writing* (Teach Yourself Books, 1983).

Peter Finch: *Between 35 and 42* (Alun Books, 1982).

Peter Finch (ed.): *Typewriter Poems* (Second Aeon/Something Else Press, 1972).

Peter Finch and Meic Stephens (eds.): *Green Horse* (Christopher Davies, 1979).

S.T. Gardiner: *The Poet's Yearbook* 1977 (Poet's Yearbook Ltd, 1977).

John Haines: *Poets on Poetry — Living off the Country — Essays on Poetry and Place* (University of Michigan Press, 1981).

Herman Hesse: *My Belief* (Panther, 1978).

Robert Hendrickson: *The Literary Life & Other Curiosities* (Penguin, 1981).

Norman Hidden: *The Poet's Guide No 2 — How to Get Your Poems Accepted* (Workshop Press, 1981).

Michael Horovitz: *Growing Up: Selected Poems 1951–79* (Allison & Busby, 1979).

Ted Hughes and Fay Goodwin: *Remains of Elmet* (Faber, 1979).

Ted Hughes and Peter Keen: *River* (Faber, 1983).

Judson Jerome: *The Poet and The Poem* (Writer's Digest Books, 1979).

Judson Jerome: *The Poet's Handbook* (Writer's Digest Books, 1980).

John D. Jump (ed.): *The Critical Idiom* (Methuen, various volumes and dates):

G.S. Fraser: *Metre, Rhyme and Free Verse*

Paul Merchant: *The Epic*

John Fuller: *The Sonnet*

John D. Jump: *The Ode*

Arnold P. Hinchliffe: *Modern Verse Drama*

Ernst Haublein: *The Stanza*

Peter Faulkner: *Modernism*

Laddie, Prescott and Vitoria: *The Modern Law of Copyright* (Butterworths, 1989)

Michael Legat: *An Author's Guide to Publishing* (Hale, 1982).

Peter Marcan: *Arts Address Book* (Peter Marcan, 1989).

Lotte Moos: *Time to be Bold* (Centerprise Trust Ltd, 1981).

Dave Morley and Ken Worpole (eds.): *The Republic of Letters — Working-Class Writing and Local Publishing* (Comedia, 1982).

Betty Mulcahy: *How To Speak A Poem* (Autolycus Press, 1987).

Pablo Neruda: *Memoirs* (Souvenir Press, 1977).

Tillie Olsen: *Silences* (Virago, 1980).

Frank S. Pepper (ed.): *Handbook of 20th-Century Quotations* (Sphere, 1984).

Robert Peters: *The Black And Blue Guide To Current Literary Journals* in 3 vols (Dustbooks, 1987).

George Plimton (ed.): *Writers at Work — The Paris Review Interviews*, 7 vols (Penguin 1977–87).

Alan Riddell (ed.): *Typewriter Art* (London Magazine Editions, 1975).

Stevie Smith: *Collected Poems* (Allen Lane, 1975).

Some Magazine: *The Some Symposium — Poets on Stage* (Release Press, 1978).

Gertrude Stein: *How to Write* (Something Else Press, 1973).

R.S. Thomas: *Between Here and Now* (Macmillan, 1981).

R.S. Thomas: *Selected Prose* (Poetry Wales Press, 1983).

Edward Uhlan: *The Rogue of Publishers' Row* (Exposition Banner, 1956).

Sir Stanley Unwin *The Truth About Publishing* (George Allen and Unwin, 1926).

Philip Ward: *A Lifetime's Reading* (Oleander Press, 1982).

Index

Abse, Dannie, 89, 96
acknowledgements, 42–3, 54, 55–6, 62
Ada Press, 61
Adastra Publishing Company, 81
Adcock, Fleur, 13, 89
advertisements, 74–5, 77
Agenda, 33, 50
agents, literary, 24, 52
Agogo Ago go, 71
Allardyce, Barnett, 50
Allen, Donald, 97
Allison and Busby, 48, 115
Alp, *see* Association of Little Presses
Alta, 45
Alun Books, 61
Ambit, 33
American Express, 85
American Poetry Review, 85
Amis, Kingsley, 54
Amra Imprint, 50
Amstrad, 21, 66, 71, 110
Anania, Michael, 10, 11
And, 33
Anderson, Elliott, 32
Anderson, Jack, 93
anthologies, 24, 30, 31, 41, 55, 57
Antaeus, 85
Antigonish Review, 85
Antioch Review, 85
Anvil, 49
Applemac, 21
Apples & Snakes, 95, 104
Aquarius, 33
arts associations, 17, 31, 36, 78, 104–5
Arts Council An Chomhairle Ealaíon, 77
Arts Council of Great Britain (ACGB),
    77, 91, 104, 111
Arts Council Poetry Library, 109
arts councils, 77–8, 90, 105–6
Arvon Foundation, 9, 88, 106–7
Association of Little Presses (ALP), 10,
    34, 50, 61, 66, 76–7, 103, 106–7, 114
Atlantic Monthly 84
Attila the Stockbroker, 92
Audio Books, 31
Aulton Press, 61
Austin Clarke Library, 109
Australia, 85
Author, The, 58, 112

Autolycus Press, 94
awards, 91

B4, 50
Balsam Flex, 70
Baker, Kenneth, 54
BB Books, 50, 61
BBC Radio, 30, 57, 58
Beasley, Paul, 104
Beckett, Samuel, 96
Bell, Robin, 109
Bennett, Arnold, 46
Bentley's Miscellany, 32
Betjeman, Sir John, 49, 101
Between Here and Now (Thomas), 43
Between 35 and 42 (Finch), 25
binding, 63, 69
Black, A. and C., 10, 24, 34, 51, 56, 114
Black, D.M., 82
Blackstaff Press, 48
Blake, William, 59, 97
Blast, 32
Bloodaxe Books, 49, 101
blood pressure, 127
Blue Cloud Quarterly, 84
Bodleian Library, 73
Bogg, 33
bookfairs, 77, 106
Book News, 107
book publication, 40–7, 48
Bookseller, The, 77
bookshops, 11, 35, 72, 75, 78
Book Trust, 85, 91, 106–7
Bridport Arts Centre, 89
British Council, 35, 114
British Library, 73
British Literary Periodicals, 35, 114
British Poetry Since 1945 (Lucie-Smith),
    97
British Telecom, 31
broadcasting, 55, 58
Brown, Andrew, 70
Brunner, John, 60
Bukowski, Charles, 44
Burns, Robert, 59
Buttrick, George F., 97
BWA, 113
Byron, Lord, 60

calendars, 31
Cambridge University Library, 73
camera ready copy, 66
Canada, 85
Canon, 68
Cape, 48
Capilano Review, 85
Carcanet, 49
cash, 57–8
Cassell, 51
Cassell and the Publishers Association Directory of Publishing, 51
cassette duplicating, 70
Catalogue of Small Press Books in Print, 51, 106, 114
Caxton, William 65, 71
Chambers' Twentieth-Century Dictionary, 20
Chapman, 33
Chatto and Windus, 48
Cheltenham Festival Poetry Competition, 89, 90
Chester Poets, 33
Childe Roland, 50
Chiron Press, 50
City Limits, 30, 95
Clarke, Gillian, 40, 113
classified ads, 31
Cobbing, Bob, 60, 68, 92, 106
Cocteau, Jean, 12
collating, 69
Collected Poems (Larkin), 64
Collection Poems (Smith), 43
Collected Poems 1955–79 (Amis), 54
Collins-Grafton-Fontana, 49
Collins Harvill, 48, 114
compact disc, 71
competitions, 9, 43, 88–90, 113
Computer Poet, 71
computers, 71
Conran, Antony, 13, 92
contents page, 62
Coordinating Council of Literary Magazines (America), 10
copies, keeping, 22, 23, 45, 86
Copinger, W.A., 56
copyright, 52–59, 62, 73
copyright libraries 53, 73
Copyright (Copinger and James), 56
Corinth Books, 99
Cornhill, 32
cover design, 68–9
covering letters, 25, 46
Crabflower Pamphlets, 61
Crafts, 31
Crazy Horse, 85

Creasey, John, 38
Creative Language, 111
creative writing classes, 94
Critical Quarterly, 32
criticism, 16–17
Crossley-Holland, Kevin, 82
Crozier, Andrew, 97
Cunliffe, David, 61
curriculum vitae, 25
Cutler, Ivor, 13, 92, 96
Cych, Leon, 110

Daily Telegraph, 29
daisy wheels, 66
Dalhousie Review, 85
Dangaroo Press, 50
Day Lewis, Cecil, 16
Deahl, James, 86
Deceptive Grin of the Gravel Porters, The (Ewart), 44
Dedalus, 50
Defoe, Daniel, 46
Dent, 48
design, 68
desk-top publishing (DTP), 67, 115
Deutsch, Andre, 48
Dial-a-poem, 31
Diamond, 50
Dick, Jill, 95
Dickinson, Emily, 40
Directory of Poetry Publishers (Fulton and Ferber), 34, 86, 114
direct selling, 76
discounts, bookshop, 72
distribution, 62, 72, 74, 78
Dr Faust's Sea-Spiral Spirit (Redgrove), 45
Doctor's Dilemma, A, 33
Donleavy, J.P., 38
Dorgan, Theo, 109
drawings, 43
Dreiser, Theodore, 46
Dubliners (Joyce), 38
duplicating, 69
Dustbooks, 34, 114

Earley, Tom, 82
Eastern Arts Association, 50
Echo Room, The, 33
Edinburgh Review, 33
Edison, 16
Edwards, Ken, 12
Eglinton, Edna, 35
Egoist, The, 32
Eisteddfod, 88
Eliot, T.S., 48, 97, 109

Encounter, 32
English Review, The, 32
English Subtitles (Porter), 45
Enitharmon Press, 49
Enright, Mary, 109
European Association for the Promotion of Poetry, 107
European Poetry Translation Prize, 111
Ewart, Gavin, 44, 89
Excess, 50
exhibitions, 77
Exposition Press, 81

Faber and Faber, 48, 64, 97
Faber Book of Contemporary American Poetry (Vendler), 97
Faber Memorial Prize, 91
Fanthorpe, U.A., 49
Fainlight, Ruth, 82
Fairfax, John, 106
Federation of Worker Writers and Community Publishers, 95, 107
Fed News, 107
Fenton, James, 49
Ferber, Ellen, 34
Fiddlehead, 85
Finlay, Ian Hamilton, 20, 60
First Time, 33
Fisher, Allen, 60
Fitzgerald, Edward, 46
Fleeting Monolith, 50
foreign publication, 84–7
Four Eyes, 50
Fowler's Modern English Usage, 23, 115
Fragmente, 33
Freelance Press Services, 34
Fugitive Pieces (Byron), 60
Fulton, Len, 34, 86
future books, 71

Gallery Press, 49
Galloping Dog Press, 50, 69
Gardiner, S.T., 33
Garlick, Raymond, 14, 24, 92
Gay Men's Press, 49
Georgia Review, 85
Gestetner, 69
Getting Your Poetry Published (Finch), 106
Ginger Man, The, (Donleavy), 38
Global Tapestry Journal, 33
Going Down Swinging, 85
Gomer Press, 48
Goodwin, Fay, 43
Gowers, Sir Ernest, 23, 115
Gowrie, Lord, 88

grants, 77–8
Graves, Robert, 40
Green Desert, The, (Webb), 45
Green Horse (Finch & Stephens), 45
Greensboro Review, 84
Greeting Card and Calendar Association, 36
greetings cards, 29
Gregory Trust Fund, E.C., 91
Grey, Zane, 46
Griffiths, Bill, 71, 106
Grosseteste Review, 106
Growing Up (Horovitz), 43
Guardian, The, 11, 29
Guest, Harry, 82
Guide to Literary Prizes, Grants and Awards, 91, 107

Hackney Writers' Workshop, 43
Haines, John, 40, 97
Hamish Hamilton, 48
Hammicks, 74
Hangman Books, 50
Hard Pressed Poetry, 50
Harnby, Cecil, 99
Harrison, Ruth, 104
Hart, David, 110
Harwood, Lee, 49
Headland, 50
Heaney, Seamus, 48, 97
Heathcote, 74
Henderson, Bill, 59
Hermes, 85
Hesse, Herman, 16
Hidden, Norman, 9, 17
Hippopotamus Press, 50
H'm (Thomas), 45
Hodgkiss, Peter, 69
Hoffman, 32
Holden, Molly, 82
Honest Ulsterman, The, 33
Hong Kong, 84, 85
Honno, 50
Hot-paper copiers, 68
How To Publish Yourself (Finch), 79, 114
How To Speak A Poem (Mulcahy), 94
Hubbard, Tom, 111
Hughes, Ted, 43, 48, 65, 88, 97, 106
humorous verse, 29
Hutchinson, 48, 64
Hutchinson Book of Post-War British Poems (Abse), 97
hype, 48

I Have No Gun But I Can Spit (Baker), 54
IBM PC, 71

illustrations, 43
Imagination on Trial, The (Burns and Sugnet), 96
India, 85
ink-jet printers, 66
In Memoriam A.H.H. (Tennyson), 9
instant print shops, 67
International Directory of Little Magazines and Small Presses, 35
International Reply Coupons (IRCs), 85, 86
International Standard Book Numbers (ISBNs), 41, 61–62
Into Print (Quilliam & Grove-Stephensen), 115
In The American Tree (Silliman), 97
introductions, 62
Iota, 33
Iron, 33, 50
ISBNs. *See* International Standard Book Numbers
italics, 22

Jandl, Ernst, 94
Jay, Peter, 82
Jenkins, Nigel, 13
Jennings, Elizabeth, 88
Jerome, Judson, 34, 86, 98
Jewasinski, Ed, 71
Jewett, Sarah Orne, 98
Joe Soap's Canoe, 33
John, Roland, 18
Johnson, B.S., 96
Johnson, Dr, 46
Johnson, Linton Kwesi, 92
Jones Family Editions, 71
Jones, Chris, 71
Jones, Elis Gwyn, 112
Jones, Glyn, 52–3
Jones, John, 61
Jones, Sally Baker, 112
Jonson, Ben, 52
Joolz, 94
Joyce, James, 38, 46

Kangaroo, 85
Keen, Peter, 43
Kenyon Review, 85
Kinzie, Mary, 32
Kite, 33
Krax, 33
Krino, 33
Kroklok, 33

Label, 33
Lady, The, 30

Landfall, 85
Landmarks, 44
language poetry, 97
Lark Lane Poetry Books, 50
Larkin, Philip, 48, 49, 64, 110
laser printers, 67
League of Canadian Poets, 86
Leaves of Grass (Whitman), 60
legal action, 56
length of poems, 24–5, 41
letterpress, 65
letters, 25, 29, 46
Letter to a Young Poet (Hesse), 16
libraries, 53, 62–3, 83, 107
Library of Cambridge University, 73
Library of Trinity College, Dublin, 73
Lifetime's Reading, A (Ward), 97
Lijn, Liliane, 13
Ling, 85
Listener, The, 29
literary agents, 24, 52
Literary Review, 29, 32
Little Magazine, The (Hoffman, Allen and Ulrich), 32
Little Magazine Collection, 108
Little Magazine in America, The, 32
little magazines 10–11, 32–35. *See also under individual titles*
Littlewood Press, 49
Living Off the Country (Haines), 97
Living Poet, The (BBC), 30
Lobby Press Newsletter, 33
Logue, Christopher, 54
London Magazine, 32
London Review of Books, 29
London School of Economics, 19
Lonely Suppers of W.V. Balloon, The (Middleton), 45
Longman, 114
Longville, Tim, 45, 97
Lucie-Smith, Edward, 97
Lume Spento, A (Pound), 60

MacCraig, Norman, 45
MacDairmid, Hugh, 52–3
McGough, Roger, 48, 49, 65, 101
Macmillan, 24, 34, 48, 114
Mainstream Publishing, 48
Malahat Review, 85
Mammon, 50
Manamead, 50
manuscript presentation 20–3, 44, 41–7
Mar, 33, 42
markets, 10, 29–36, 48–51, 84–7
Mastercard, 86
Mathias, Roland, 113

Mattoid, 85
Maypole Editions, 85
Meanjin Quarterly, 85
Melville, Herman, 46
Memoirs (Neruda), 45
Michael, Amanda L., 56
microfiche, 71
Middleton, Christopher, 45
Miller, David, 107
mimeo revolution, 69
Mir Poets, 50
Mitchell, Adrian, 88, 89, 92
Moat, John, 106
modernists, 97
Modern Law of Copyright, 56
Mole, John, 82
Momentum, 33, 38
Moorcock, Michael, 97
Moore, Geoffrey, 97
Moos, Lotte, 42–3
Morgan, Edwin, 13, 89
Morning Star, 50
Morris, William, 60
Morrison, Blake, 96
Moss Rose Books, 61
Motion, Andrew, 49
Mottram, Eric, 60, 96
Mulcahy, Betty, 94
Munday and Slatter, 60

National Book League, 106
National Convention of Poets and Small Presses, 108
National Library of Scotland, 73
National Library of Wales, 73
National Poetry Competition, 88, 110
National Poetry Secretariat, 111
Necessity for Atheism, The (Shelley), 59
Neighbours, 11
Neruda, Pablo, 45
New British Poetry, 49, 97
New England Review, 85
New Prospects, 33
newspapers, 29, 57
New Statesman, 29
new technology, 66, 67
New Voices, 85
New Welsh Review, 33
New Yorker, 84, 85
New York Quarterly, 85
New Zealand, 85
nom de plume, 43
North, The, 33, 110
North & South, 50
North Dakota Quarterly, 85
Northern Arts Poetry Library, 108

Northern Irish Arts Council, 77
Northwest Review, 85
Numbers, 33
Nuttall, Jeff, 50

Oasis, 33
Observer, 29, 88
offset-litho, 65, 68
Old Maps and New, (MacCaig), 45
Oleander, 50, 97
Olsen, Tillie, 15, 89
Olson, Charles, 13
Orbis, 33, 35, 38, 91
Ore, 33
Oriel Bookshop, 10, 35, 89, 102, 108, 114
origination, 65
Orme, David 111
Otter, 33
Outposts, 18, 33, 38, 82
Overdue Books, 61
overseas markets 84–7
Oxford University Press, 24, 48

page make up, 67
Paladin, 49, 97
PALPI – *Poetry And Little Press Information*, 34, 50, 51, 86, 106
Paris Review Interviews, 15
Painted Bride Quarterly, 85
Password, 108
Pauper's Press, 61
payment 57–8
Penguin, 49, 96, 97, 114
Penguin Book of American Verse (Moore), 97
Penguin Book of Contemporary British Poetry (Morrison & Motion), 96
Pennine Platform, 33
Pen:Umbra, 34
People to People, 36
"Perfect" (MacDairmid), 52
performance, 70
permissions, 55–6
Peterloo Poets, 49
Phoenix Review, 85
photocopying, book production by, 68
photocopies, keeping, 22, 23, 26, 45, 86
Pi, 107
Pig, 50
Piker's Pad, 70
Pitt-Kethley, Fiona, 48, 101
plagiarism, 52–3
Planet, 34
Play the Piano Drunk Like a Percussion Instrument Until the Fingers Begin to Bleed a Bit (Bukowski, 44

PN Review, 12, 33
Poe, Edgar Allan, 60, 74
Poems By The Way (Morris), 60
Poems, Chiefly in the Scottish Dialect (Burns), 59
Poems on Various Occasions (Byron), 60
Poet and Printer, 50
Poet Laureate, 9
Poetmeat, 107
Poetry (Hong Kong), 85
Poetry (USA), 42, 85, 92
Poetry Association of Scotland, 109
Poetry Australia, 85
Poetry Book Society, 109
Poetry Business, 109
Poetry Canada, 85
Poetry Chicago, 84
Poetry Durham, 33
Poetry East, 85
Poetry Ireland, 109
Poetry Ireland Review, 33, 42, 109
Poetry Kanto, 85
Poetry Library, The, 91, 95, 103, 108, 109–110
Poetry Listing, 110
Poetry London Newsletter, 110
Poetry Markets For Canadians, 86
Poetry Nippon, 85
Poetry Now (BBC), 30
Poetry Olympics, 33, 94
Poetry Review, 33, 35, 38, 42, 111
Poetry Society, 17, 18, 35, 83, 91, 95, 108, 110–111
Poetry Store, 108
Poetry Travels, 111
Poetry Wales, 33, 84
Poetry Wales Press, 49
Poet's Market (Jerome), 34, 86, 114
Poets on Stage: The Some Symposium, 93
Poet's Voice, 33
Poet's Yearbook, 33
Pollinger, Laurence, 95
Porter, Peter, 45
postage, 45, 85–6
postcards, 31
posters, 31, 89
Postmoderns, The: The New American Poetry Revised (Allen and Buttrick), 97
Post Office, 71
Pound, Ezra, 16, 60, 92, 96, 97
Prairie Fire, 85
Prairie Schooner, 85
Prakalpana, 85
prayer, 96
Prebendal, 50

presentation of manuscripts, 20–3, 39, 41–7
press releases, 74
Prest Roots Press, 61
previous publication, 25–6, 42, price, 72
print, 20
print run, 64
Printer's Devil, 34, 36
printing processes, 65–6
Print Out, 50
private presses, 65
Professional Magnetics Ltd., 70
pseudonyms, 43
Psychopoetica, 33
"publications received" pages, 34, 86
publicity, 33, 74
Public Lending Right, 41, 108
publishers, commercial, 45, 46, 48–51
Publish It Yourself (Finch), 106
Publish It Yourself and Make It Pay (Templeton), 70
Publishers Association, 51, 55, 57
Pyrofiche, 71

Quartos, 91, 111
Quarry, 85
quotation 55–6

Raddle Moon, 85
radio, 30–1
Rank Xerox, 68
Ransford, Tess, 111
Rattle Bag, The (Hughes and Heaney), 97
Ratushinskaya, Irina, 48
Raven Arts, 50
Raworth, Tom, 49
Re-Verb, 61
Reading, Peter, 82
readings, 17, 58, 92–5
Reality Studios, 12
recording, 31
records, keeping, 24, 47
Redgrove, Peter, 14, 19, 38, 45, 49, 97
Red Sharks Press, 50
Reed, Jeremy, 49
reference books, 9, 10, 15, 22–3, 24, 34–5, 51, 56, 77, 86–7, 91, 114–5
Regional Arts Associations (RAAs), 17, 31, 35, 78, 83, 90, 91, 94, 104
regional verse, 31
rejection, 27, 37–39
Remains of Elmet (Keen), 43
reports, publisher's, 46
reprints, 48
retail price, 72
reviews and review copies, 74, 78, 98

revising, 23, 98
Rhinoceros, 34
Rialto, 34
River (Hughes), 43
Rogue of Publisher's Row, The (Uhlan), 81
Roneo, 69
royalties, 57
Rubayat of Omar Khayyam, The (Fitzgerald), 46

sales campaign, 74–77
Salmagundi, 85
Salmon, The, 34, 87
Sansom, Peter, 109
Saxon Ltd., 67
SBN. *See* International Standard Book Numbers
Scannell, Vernon, 14, 115
Scarp, 85
Schmidt, Michael, 12
Schools' Poetry Association, 111
Schools' Poetry Review, 111
Scripsi, 85
Scottish Arts Council, 18, 77
Scottish Association for the Speaking of Verse, 109
Scottish Poetry Library, 111
Secker and Warburg, 48, 64
Second Aeon, 7, 22, 27, 107
Selected Prose (Thomas), 39
self-publishing, 63–83
Seren Books, 49
Sergeant, Howard, 18, 82
sending work in, 24–28
Seneca Review, 85
setting text, 66–7
Seven Elephants and One Eye (Longville), 45
Shameless Hussy, The (Alta), 45
Shell Young Poet of the Year, 111
Shelley, 59
Shields, Mike, 38
Shuttle, Penelope, 14
Signal Poetry Award, 90
Silences (Olsen), 89–90
Silkin, Jon, 60
Silliman, Ron, 97
Sillitoe, Alan, 82, 93
Silver, Jeremy, 39
Simmons, James, 13, 98
simultaneous submission, 25
Sinclair, Iain, 49
Sissay, Lem, 94
Sisson, C.H., 13, 38, 39, 92
Slow Dancer, 33

Smail, A.T., 73
small presses, 49–50, 61
Small Press Group (SPG), 51, 66, 77, 112, 114
Small Presses in the UK and Ireland. An Address List, 35, 51, 108, 114
Small Press Monthly, 112
Small Press Yearbook, 51, 112, 114
Smart, Pat, 107
Smith/Doorstop, 50, 110
Smith, Ken, 98
Smith, Stevie, 43
Smith, W.H., 111
Soar, Geoffrey, 107
Society of Authors, 55, 57, 91, 112
Something Else Press, 22
song lyrics, 82
Songs of Innocence (Blake), 59
Sotheby's, 88
Sound-Text experimentation, 70
South Africa, 85
South Bank Centre, 109, 110
spacing, 22
Spare Rib, 30
specialist periodicals, 30
Spectacular Diseases, 33
Spectator, 29
Sphere, 114
Spineless Books, 61
spirit duplicating, 69
spoken-word recordings, 31
Spokes, 34
Stallworthy, John, 88
Stand, 33
Standard Book Numbering Agency, 61
Standard Book Numbers (SBNs), 41, 61–2
staplers, 69
Stephens, Meic, 45
Stone, Bernard, 102
Strange Mathematics, 39
Strength Beyond Bingo, 33
Stride, 50
Strong, Patience, 65
submitting work, 24–28, 45–47, 85–87
subscribing to magazines, 26, 34
subsidies, 32, 49, 82
Sulfur, 85
Sun, The, 11
Sunday Telegraph, 29
Sunday Times, 29
Sweet and Maxwell, 56

Tak Tak Tak, 70
talent, 16
Taliesin Trust, 112

Tamerlane, (Poe), 60
tape-recording, 20, 31
Taxus, 50
Tears In The Fence, 33
telephone poems, 20, 31
television, 30, 31
Templeton, Ian, 70
Tennyson, 9
Tenth Decade, 33
Themerson, Stephan, 9
themes, 44
Thomas, D.M., 82
Thomas, Dylan, 12, 44, 94, 111
Thomas, Ifor, 113
Thomas, Kevin, 113
Thomas, R. S., 39, 43, 45
Thornes, Stanley, Ltd., 111
Tiger Bay Books, 61
Time Out, 30, 91, 94
Times, The, 29
Times Literary Supplement, The, 32
Time To Be Bold (Moos), 42
title-page, 45, 46, 54
title-page verso, 54, 62–3
titles, 22, 44–5, 61
Tlaloc, 107
Toad's Damp Press, 50
translations, 48, 111
Trinity College, Dublin, Library, 73
TriQuarterly, 85
Tripp, John, 14
Turner, Barry, 34
typing, 21–2
typesetting, 66–7
Typesetting from Author's Disk, 67
Typewriter Poems, 22

Uhlan, Edward, 81
Ulianow, Igor, 81
Ulrich, 32
UNESCO, 41
Unfold, 85
Unidentified Flying Printer, 61
University College London Library, 108
university magazines, 84–5
University of Nebraska, 85
University of Oregon, 85
Unmuzzled Ox, 85
Unwin Hyman, 48
Unwin, Sir Stanley, 43
Upstream, 85

Val Baker, Denys, 33
vanity presses, 25, 31, 79–80
Various Art, A (Crozier and Longville), 97

Vendler, Helen, 97
Venue, 30
Verse, 33
Virago Press, 49
Visa, 86
Vital Signs (Wallace), 97
Voices Israel, 85
Vonna-Mitchell, Eric, 70

waiting, 27, 45
Wales, 45
Wallace, Ronald, 97
Wantling, William, 69
Ward, Philip, 97
Way Back to Ruthin (Jones), 61
Webb, Harri, 45
weeklies, 29, 57
Wellsweep Press, 50
Welsh Academy, 112–3
Welsh Arts Council, 10, 31, 77
Welsh Union of Writers, 113
Westerly, 85
Weyfarers, 33
What's happening, 30
Whiterose Literary Magazine, 34
Whitman, Walt, 49, 60
Wide Skirt, The, 34
Wilentz, Ted, 99
Wood Wind Publications, 110
Woman and Home, 30
women's magazines, 30
Women's Press, 49
word processors, 21, 22, 66
Wordsworth, William, 49
worker writer groups, 94–5
Works, The, 34, 118
Workshop New Poetry, 9
workshop's, writer's, 17, 92–95
Writers' and Artists' Yearbook, 10, 24, 34, 46, 51, 91, 114
writer's circles, 94–5
Writer's Circles (Dick), 94
Writer's Digest Books, 34, 114
Writers Forum, 50, 68, 69
Writers' Guild of Great Britain, 112
Writer's Handbook, 24, 34, 36, 51, 91, 114
Writer's Newsletter, 112
Writing For The BBC, 30, 36

X-Calibre, 33

Yeats, W.B., 49

Zanzibar Productions, 50
Zephania, Benjamin, 92
Zymergy, 85

126